What Happens When They Don't Grow Back

The upside down view of life after a bilateral mastectomy

Peta-Ann Wood

What Happens When They Don't Grow Back:
The upside down view of life after a bilateral mastectomy
Copyright © 2022 by Peta-Ann Wood

Tellwell Talent
www.tellwell.ca

ISBN
978-0-2288-7934-3 (Hardcover)
978-0-2288-7933-6 (Paperback)
978-0-2288-7935-0 (eBook)

Images:
Black & White post-mastectomy images by Mel Watt; Mel
Watt Photography melwattphotography.com.au

Other images supplied by Peta-Ann Wood.
PeAchy the Owl designed by Wendy James, Black Jam Graphic Design

Disclaimer
Please note that much of this publication is based on personal experience
and anecdotal evidence. Although the author and publisher have made every
reasonable attempt to achieve complete accuracy of content, they assume no
responsibility for errors or omissions. Also, you should use this information as you
see fit, and at your risk. Your particular situation may not be suited to the examples
and guidance illustrated here; you should adjust your use of the information
and recommendations accordingly. Meant to inform and entertain the reader;
nothing in this book should replace legal, medical or other professional advice.
Any trademarks, service marks, product names or named features are assumed
to be the property of their respective owners and are used for reference
only. There is no implied endorsement if we use one of these terms.

Dedication

To all the . . .

Elegantly rebellious bilateral mastectomy women who have discovered our breasts don't magically grow back . . .

Together we will be visible.

Preface

I'm Peta-Ann—often called P-A—and this is my story. Well, part of it. In 2015, I underwent a bilateral mastectomy as the main component of my treatment for early-stage breast cancer. I was forty-five at the time.

When I started treatment, the focus, post-bilateral-mastectomy, was on undergoing reconstruction as soon as possible to be able to feel normal again.

Gratefully, in Australia in 2015, and now, reconstruction is a choice, unlike some other countries, where it was and still is a pre-determined component of your treatment plan.

Cut to 2022 and the Aesthetically Flat Closure (AFC) movement is gaining incredible traction worldwide. It is sad we needed a 'movement' to advocate for a woman's choice in how she/they present to the world post-mastectomy; however I, for one, am incredibly grateful.

AFC is a valid choice, and it's now being made easier by discussions happening between patients prior to undergoing a mastectomy and treatment teams. Making the determination to stay flat does affect the actual mastectomy procedure. For those of us who didn't have, or didn't know to have, these conversations prior to our mastectomy, choosing to stay flat may also mean more surgery to remove the excess skin left for reconstruction purposes, or even an explant post-reconstruction – meaning having your implants removed. The research and options being presented through the inclusion of AFC as a viable option are amazing. Some surgeons in the United States, where the AFC movement is prevalent, even discuss various scar styles: straight, smiles, s-shape or even anchors.

As someone who has moving ribs among the consequences of my bilateral mastectomy and revision, it is also exciting to see the research being undertaken around these various scar styles and the physical impact they have on your whole body.

These are exciting times, and I greatly appreciate all the work being achieved by groups such as Not Wearing a Shirt and Stand Tall AFC to further validate our personal choice to stay flat.

If you need a push forward to assist in making your decision to stay flat or not, read on. Follow your heart, your gut, your soul, your intuition—whatever speaks to you about what's best.

Celebrating uniqueness,
Peta-Ann

Acknowledgements

It takes a village. I am forever grateful for all those who have been part of mine. You have all filled my world with joy, love, light, laughter, silliness and knowledge. Thank you.

Extra tzzuzy love 'n' light goes to Craig, Spike, Cass, Liz, Kath, Jaz, Trudy, Kel, Lorna, Lou, Casey, Mel, Suzanne, Rae and Lyn. You have all played an amazing part in my muddling and I wouldn't be here without all of you. I am forever grateful.

Much love goes to Mum and Dad. And to the greater Wood and Harvey/Nicholson/Austin clans. Thank you for your acceptance and insider knowledge.

An extra-special thank you to Linda, Melinda, Katya and Carmel for keeping me on track and laughing for the past seven years.

And finally, to my heart and soul, The Magus and The Pen. No words can describe other than plus 1 x EndGame, plus1.

Table of Contents

Be authentic. Your breasts don't define you. Your lack of breasts don't define you. Society doesn't get to tell you how to feel like a woman. that's the job of your authentic beautiful soul.

Introduction: What truly is normal?

A few years ago, I got me a-thinking . . . what does happen when your breasts don't magically grow back after a bilateral mastectomy? Will you ever be viewed by society as normal? How did your ability to choose the best path for you vanish? Why do we consistently ignore our intuition and gut feelings when we go through trauma? Such ponderings have led me on one very interesting path. Grab a cuppa and let's have a gander at life upside down after a bilateral mastectomy.

First things first. What is this word 'normal'? Who defines it really? I grabbed one of my many versions of the Oxford Dictionary—yes, I have a few—and it is an adjective which means 'conforming to standard, usual, regular, ordinary'. So why is everyone so hell-bent on feeling *normal*? It truly is such a benign word.

I've known since birth that I didn't fit into the society-accepted version of *normal*. You know, when you don't fit in because you're always too *something*. For me, I was too big, too tall, too smart, feet too big, breasts way too big, hair too thick or too curly . . . the list goes on. To quote my younger brother, 'Not fitting in with society's version of normal is exactly how I fit in.'

I chose at an early age to not subscribe to what someone else's opinion of *normal* was. For me, I choose to be elegantly unique, stylish and authentic, and, as an introvert, to keep much of my thinking inside my head. Until now, that is.

To set the scene, I'm living well, with and beyond breast cancer. I was diagnosed a couple of months prior to my forty-sixth birthday, and my initial surgical treatment was a bilateral mastectomy and lymph node removal. I have subsequently chosen to 'stay-flat', meaning no prosthesis, no reconstruction, and very concave ribs, or *divots*, if you will.

This was my educated choice of what was best for me. I am highly supportive of everyone's individual choices in this space, whether you choose to have reconstruction, wear prosthesis or none of the above. It's your choice, your decision, and, quite frankly, no one else's business.

I am also hugely supportive of all the associated healthcare providers and charities assisting breast cancer survivors and mastectomy recipients to find their feet again, whatever their version of normal is: flat, prosthesis or reconstruction.

What I am not supportive of is the focus on what society dictates is required for women to feel *normal* again. After a mastectomy, this somehow equals having reconstruction or wearing prosthesis. No other option equates to *normal*, according to almost every media report I have ever read or seen. Even reading some recent research into reconstruction, I discovered I allegedly have more mental-health issues because I haven't had reconstruction. I think you'll find my response to that would be: '*Really?*'

And then there's the clinicians who refer to my rolled-under, concave ribs as a deformity, and reconstruction should fix them. Once again, I am deemed *not normal*. However, at no point is the definition of *normal* questioned. At no point is an alternative version of *normal* portrayed. At no point is anyone asked where their version of *normal* comes from, or why it's important to them. It is simply assumed being female equals breasts equals normal, for everyone.

I have decided to rebel against this version of normal, quietly and definitively. This decision came after much soul-searching, trial and error, ignoring my inner-knowing and intuition, succumbing, and discovering the really odd things that may occur to your mind, body and spirit after having a bilateral mastectomy.

This is my story, my lived experience along with some of the components of the 'ways and means act' I have instigated to fulfil my peaceful version of uniqueness for *me*, not society.

I truly look forward to the day when we all celebrate our individual uniqueness and won't be stuck in a society-induced pattern of *normal* based on gender-assigned physical attributes.

Before you head down the 'I want to be normal' path, ask yourself, What's best for me? Celebrate you as a person. Honour you as a person. Respect you as a person. Love you as a person. That's your version of normal. It really is that simple for me.

Now. In the words of the Narrator from *The Rocky Horror Picture Show*, 'I'd like, if I may, to take you on a strange journey ...' Well, a strange *odyssey*, actually.

Am I more than a walking pair of breasts?

I celebrate uniqueness. I celebrate personal style. I'm not that great at celebrating normal. Or, as I have established, conforming to society's version of normal. Elegance and grace capture my attention, not normality.

Very early on in my recovery odyssey, while working out how to live the best version of me going forward, the concept of regaining my 'new normal' was all I heard. As a sidebar, the term 'new normal' has been a part of bilateral-mastectomy-recovery parlance for a very long time, the COVID-19 pandemic didn't come up with that one.

I initially embraced the search for my new normal, as I knew I couldn't go backwards. Never been one to hang out in the past, me. I also knew I was searching for something more than normal. This search took me many places, down many rabbit holes, and what I can share now is for me, it's not *normal* I need, it's rediscovering my uniqueness, style, grace and authenticity, all with a wee bit of quirkiness thrown in for good measure.

Every now and then we are presented with life situations which challenge our status quo, how we perceive ourselves and how we feel society perceives us. Sometimes we allow these life challenges and situations to define our confidence in our personal style.

the fact that I didn't fit in with society's version of normal is exactly how I fit in.

One such challenge is suddenly becoming a youngish bilateral mastectomy chick—an amputee, if you will. This sends all sorts of what I refer to as crazy fruit-loop thoughts tumbling through your brain at all hours of the day and night, banishing your personal style and confidence to the back burner, potentially for good, as you simply have too much 'important stuff' to navigate while undergoing treatment regimens.

As a generalisation, society seems to focus on the notion women must have breasts to be deemed as a bona fide female, and in some circles we must have ample cleavage. In Australia, it would appear we are obsessed with breasts. According to The Northland Age Editor, Myjanne Jensen, in a breast implant feature for *ABC Radio National*, research showed breast augmentation is the most popular cosmetic surgery in Australia. As an example, 20,000 procedures were undertaken in 2018. The larger the better, apparently. Please note, this is a generalisation, and yet one that is rarely challenged publicly.

Prior to my diagnosis and bilateral mastectomy, I fell into the incredibly ample cleavage category. And despite the immenseness of the girls (to give you a visual, my younger brother recently made this observation about my former cleavage: 'They would arrive in the room five minutes before your face'), I have truly never understood why a pair of functional mammary glands defined me as a female member of society. Why do women with smaller breasts feel the need to have augmentation and enhancements? And who determines what is small or large in the first place? Can they not simply just be breasts?

Post-mastectomy, these questions seem to become even more relevant during the barrage of treatment and life-decision points. But changing the societal norm from one of 'women equals breasts' to one of acceptance and valuing overall beauty as opposed to external shape is one of those age-old, idealistic, head-in-the-clouds desires.

In the early days of my diagnosis and treatment, I had a truly disturbing yet positive life-changing moment. It was Breast Cancer Awareness Month 2015, and I was driving back home from one of my first oncology physiotherapy appointments. I was a newbie to the breast cancer scene and was so excited to see a tradies ute all decked out in breast-cancer-pink supporters' paraphernalia, and then I saw the sign on the back windscreen: save the boobs.

I pulled a recoiling *WTAF?* face, thankful for my car's dark-tinted windows. Save the boobs? Are they not attached to a woman whose life is vital with or without them? My boobs are no longer attached to me, but they're in storage somewhere, in pieces, in a lab, just in case comparative testing is required down the track. Is this what they meant? I think not.

This was a huge wow moment for me, and once again I started to think. I recognise that the sexualisation of breasts in general, breast cancer awareness, and the even greater issue of women being less valued by society based on the size of her breasts are not things I can change overnight.

However, I can pose questions and cause disruption that will place greater emphasis on the acceptance of uniqueness, and developing a greater understanding of the self-esteem, self-worth and self-confidence issues many women endure based on the size, shape and sexualisation of breasts. Perhaps some of our self-esteem and self-confidence issues may lessen if we thought a wee bit differently about the importance of breasts within society, from an aesthetic point of view, and realise that we, as women, are simply enough, mind, body and soul.

So to find this acceptance and valuing of women, where do we start disrupting society, rebelling against the accepted social norm of women equals breasts?

Disruption starts with understanding the choices available and standing up for your personal values. If you're not aware of your personal values, I strongly recommend taking the time to figure them out. They are your anchor point for all your choices and decision-making. Life becomes just that wee bit simpler to navigate when you are able to ask yourself if a choice or decision is in alignment with, or goes against, your values. Mine are quite simple. The top five are: respect, acceptance, uniqueness, playfulness and grace.

Through understanding my personal values, I was able to make the best odyssey-based choices for me. They give me the structure I need to push back against our society's emphasis on breasts, to rebel against the underlying sexualisation and the non-acceptance of *different*. They give me the courage to share my experience and thoughts, which may assist you to find your voice and share with the world what your version of normal or, dare I say, uniqueness will be.

Source Unknown

Superhero status: before and after

I read an article not long after my bilateral about the suffering of ladies with enormous breasts. This article simply captured the essence of my life . . . well, the former version of my life. Low self-esteem, hiding, never going out, carrying weight, all because I disliked my breasts and the world loved them. I was never Peta-Ann, I was the 'chick with the huge boobs', a walking shelf, even.

An extremely rare photo of the Shelf. My 45th birthday, completely unaware that, by my next birthday, they would be gone.

My life was about doing everything I could to hide my breasts. Working in a male-dominated environment—alpha-male, at that—was challenging every day. I often jested I should get my breasts tattooed, the top of my right breast stating, EYES ABOVE, and on the left breast, LET ME KNOW IF THEY ANSWER BACK. Moving into the IT environment was even worse. In IT, the stereotypical man-child, and occasional female, seemed to forget I had eyes. If I actually wore clothes that fit me (i.e., showed I had a waist), I swear that, in their eyes, I morphed into a Japanese anime figure, the most commonly sought-after at comicon events.

Society deemed that my large breasts were amazing and should be revered, but at no point did anyone ever ask me what the emotional affect was on me from all the stares and comments, let alone the physical issues.

I remember vividly three occasions in a former workplace where the situation evoked a feeling of sheer aggravation within me. I am a self-professed needer of harmony in all environments and avoider of confrontation of all kinds, let alone a runner away from violence, so these situations were pretty horrendous.

One was a ten-minute conversation where at no point did my male colleague look up from my cleavage to address me eye-to-eye, and at the next meeting with him, his opening statement was to tell me he liked the colour of my bra. The next incident—another which definitely constitutes sexual harassment—was a male co-worker phoning me and starting the conversation by seriously asking me for my bra size and then suggesting I could provide him with sexual favours instead of including him in a project team. That one I did report. He's no longer working for the company. The final incident was at a social event. One of the male bosses decided it was okeh to say, 'I'd do those,' while standing next to me and nodding at my breasts. Now, this particular gent had never spoken to me professionally or otherwise, despite working with me for a number of years, and never acknowledged my work, but for some reason decided it was okeh to say *that* to a group of male colleagues whom I worked with daily. I truly felt the need to slap him down physically and metaphorically; however, I am grateful I know that lowering my energetic vibration wouldn't make me any better than him.

Sadly, these were not isolated incidents. Just the top three, really. And even more sadly, I did not feel confident or worthy enough to challenge the voicer of any these opinions and just kept letting them slide. All I can do now is apologise to any other women who have had to endure such comments and behaviour because I was not brave enough at the time to stand up. I am now.

Being the owner of enormous cleavage has many physical challenges. Surprisingly, I didn't have shoulder issues until after my mastectomy—go figure. However, as well as the sheer weight of my excessively large breasts, their hideousness during summer (never being able to wear anything sleeveless, let alone off the shoulder; the heat rash; and clothes never fitting properly), I also had to contend with the constant leering.

A short digression. When I bought clothes off the rack to fit my cleavage, they would be way too big in the shoulders, underarms, and waist, and typically would make me appear pregnant. Apparently, for fashion houses, as a female you can have a big stomach and be short, but you can't be tall, have a waist and huge breasts. The word 'matronly' was used in the article I read that morning—I cannot come up with a better word. And don't get me started on the hideous undergarments.

This is just a small précis of the less than positives during my life with big breasts. Is it any wonder that I'd wanted a breast reduction since my mid-twenties?

On the flipside, huge breasts do have superhuman powers. They saved me from scalding coffee, and it turns out that when they decided they might be a source of death, their enormousness may have also saved me.

How is it they have superhuman powers, you ask? Some may say it was the 'romantic' attention I received due to my cleavage, I say see the aforementioned sexual harassment statements and this was my daily life. In fact, I preferred any potential suitor to not be enamoured with my breasts . . . a ridiculous expectation, but I did live in hope!

To start with, there's the scalding-coffee incident. It was hilarious. Picture this: two incredibly intelligent women, both tall, both with large breasts, mine definitely bigger. The scenario commences like any other morning at work. The most vital meeting of the morning: the first coffee run. My colleague and I wandered down the two flights of stairs to reach the company's internal café. We ordered our takeaway coffees, hamming it up as we normally do with a number of folks, as were well known in the building. We meandered out of the café. The floor on which the café is situated had a deck area outside—you know the drill: tables and chairs, etc. While we were in the café, this outside area had filled up with numerous new company recruits; it was obviously a marshalling point for a visit to the big top. We walked out just past the recruits, heading for the stairs. I was carrying my coffee in my left hand, my colleague was carrying hers in her left too, and she was on my left side. Just as we moved past the recruits to the fork in the road between the stairs and the lift, my colleague stated, 'Let's use the lift,' and pointed with her right hand.

Now, the recruits were directly behind me and wouldn't have seen the amazing scene which unfolded. As she pointed in the direction of the lift, she thwacked my cup, which left my hand and travelled upwards about ten centimetres, then landed squarely on my shelf (a common term used to describe my breasts). Nary a drop of coffee had left the cup at this point. There it was, the full-to-the-brim long black teetering on my breast shelf. I swiftly grasped for the cup, and this was the only time any of the scalding liquid left it—damn me for drinking black coffee. Luckily it was only a small trickle, which left the cup as I physically removed it from my shelf.

By this stage, my colleague was standing directly in front of me, hunched down, her head appearing to be in my cleavage, loudly exclaiming, 'They're farkin' awesome!' Fits of laughter ensued. Even now, years down the track, peals of laughter are achieved when reminiscing. Now for the really funny bit: all the company newbies could see was one senior female officer leaning into the bosom of another tall, super-buxom chick, simply exclaiming what she thought of my breasts, as opposed to the reality of being in awe of my breasts for saving me from scalding-hot coffee. Welcome to the company, folks!

Unfortunately, their next use of the superhero status wasn't quite as hilarious.

Let's backtrack to November 2014. While at a conference in Canberra, I found a lump in my right breast. It was a freak-out moment, but, ever the pragmatist, I set up a doc's appointment for when I returned to Brisneyland.

On my arrival back to Brisbane, the night of a particularly devastating storm (another 'something's brewing' moment) I popped off and did all the ensuing doctor's examinations and ultrasounds. Not my first; in fact, I'd found my first lump and was tested at twenty-three, so I wasn't too worried.

Results back and they were all clear. Although I particularly loved the radiographer's report, which stated I had extremely large breasts and this made diagnosis difficult. When I read this, I was overcome with sarcasm. I felt like they had made a discovery: I had extremely large breasts. Well done. Brilliant deduction. Clearly, I hadn't noticed this, ever. But at the same time, I was kind of, 'Hmmm . . . well, if having large breasts makes detection more difficult, what are you doing about it? You're the scientist, I was born this way.'

All clear results. Excellent, I thought. Yay. Life back on track. Only a small deviation. I told my boss after the fact, and didn't tell anyone else except my younger brother and a close mate. No one else knew.

So off I toddled with life. But my intuition was nagging me. I decided it was the toxic relationship I found myself in—another 'why am I doing this to myself' moment, but thankfully the universe took charge of that and the relationship ended abruptly in March 2015. Unbeknownst to me at the time, I couldn't have been in a better situation with him walking out.

About this time I was chatting with my naturopath, and I mentioned to her I was bleeding from the left nipple and asked what I should do about it. Her response: 'Doctor. Now. And accept nothing less than a referral to a breast surgeon and an ultrasound. Don't panic. It should be okeh. Probably just cysts.' Okily-dokily, and off I pop to make another appointment with my GP.

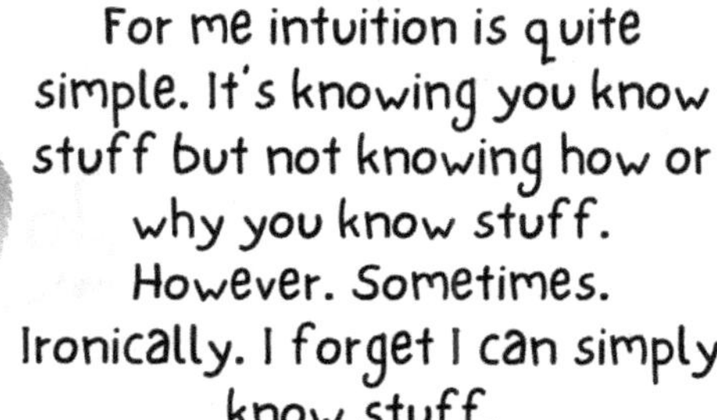

My GP didn't send me for yet another ultrasound. I'd had two in the past six months and they were clear. He thought it would probably end up being a skin disease, but sent me off to a breast and endocrine specialist, just to be safe. Enter the most fabulous and intuitive female surgeon, stage left.

It's early June 2015. My first appointment with my surgeon was interesting. Well, that was her word for me. It turns out that, in the world of breast cancer, *interesting* is not a good thing. Apparently, I was too young to be presenting the symptoms I had. She took a blood sample, gave me a handwritten list of possibilities and treatments and sent me off for more ultrasounds and a 3D mammogram. Oh, goodie, my first mammogram. At forty-five. But on her list of possibilities, there was a 3 percent chance of it being anything nasty. Excellent. No point in worrying. Can't change it either way. This became my catch phrase for the next month.

As I was not working to my normal incredibly high standards and taking days off left, right and centre, I decided to tell my bosses the reason why. They were incredibly supportive and just wanted me to get it all sorted. I still hadn't told my parents what was going on. My younger brother knew, only because this all started to unfold while he was visiting Brisbane for his birthday. For some bizarre reason, May 20—his birthday—is an angst-causing day in our family. There was a time when our mum would be made redundant from whatever job she was in on May 20—three times, in fact. Another intuition-clanging moment. And from a need-to-know basis, I'd shared with two of my work team, so they understood why I was MIA physically and emotionally—oh, and intellectually, most days!

Off I trundled to the breast centre. Three different clinicians and a visiting Sister from Indonesia poked and prodded my breasty dumplings for three hours that morning—another sign of things to come, really. I had to explain to each of them that they weren't looking for lumps per se: my symptoms were bleeding from the nipple this time. They finally understood when my breast started to bleed profusely from all the mammogram squashing, the 3D imaging machine freezing every time we needed to take lateral images of my right breast. Two rounds of ultrasounds, just to be sure, due to the size of my breasts making it difficult to see anything. Again.

I was in the dressing room when they brought in my films to take back to my surgeon. They couldn't find anything amiss, so 'You'll be okeh,' they said.

Then came the waiting for results, my favourite thing—*not*. Feeling somewhat perplexed and very much over the smallness of other people's alleged issues, I was doing what I do: working extra hours to make sure deadlines were met and information was shared appropriately. I was in a meeting with the aforementioned alpha-males when I missed the first call from my surgeon. I rang her back. My cytology results were in: all clear. The next phone call was to tell me the scans were all clear, but, 'You're too young to be this interesting,' so appointment made to come in and discuss options.

So there I was, once again in surgeon's room having the 'you're interesting' conversation. We decided a microductectomy was the way forward to determine cause and resolution. I ask when. She says I have time. 'Here's three dates: in two days' time, next week, the week after … but you have time.' I laughed. I chose June 24 as, 'I have deadlines,' which meant that two days wasn't enough notice. Yes, work was more important. And the last date was Dad's birthday. Not fair on Dad for Mum to be staying with me the night of his birthday. The first surgery date was set. As I was leaving, my surgeon said, 'Good luck with those deadlines,' in an 'interesting choice' tone. Poignant or what?

I now had a surgery date. Couldn't hide this from the Bears (Mum and Dad). This was the day I finally told my parents what had been going on.

The next day I trundled back to work to meet those deadlines. By lunchtime the following day I'd had the epiphany: *This is my life I'm playing with—who cares about deadlines!* Then we got the news: the son of one of our colleagues had been killed in a house fire. Life is way too short to be stuffing around, so I worked towards finishing up as soon as possible to take a couple of weeks' leave to have the surgery and recover. As soon as this decision was made, work requests started pouring in. The universe is funny like that. Another test for me to decide what was more important, my health and well-being or my job. And although it took another three days in the office, and I was still working from home up until the morning before my first round of surgery, I did choose me. The first small step towards making choices for my overall well-being. A new day was dawning.

Very early Wednesday morning, June 24, I jumped in a cab and headed in to have my microductectomy. Heading into theatre, the last conversation with my surgeon ended with the three outcomes: 'Clear, so nothing to worry about. Atypical and I'll have watch you for a couple of years. And nasty, which we'll need to have a conversation about,' to which we both simultaneously said, 'We won't be having that conversation.' How wrong we were.

Surgery went to plan. Was out by lunchtime Wednesday, which I was very excited about. I'd never successfully achieved day surgery before. Great anaesthetist! Home to Mum looking after me the first night and day.

My world was slowly coming back together. I felt an incredible sense of calm. It was Saturday morning, June 27.

My work sent me a lovely collection of flowering plants as a get-well gesture. I was over the moon, particularly as I am not a cut-flower kinda person—it's sort of plant murder to me. I sent thank-you texts to my boss and everyone, had silly conversations with my BFF about new business ventures—flower-pot delivery with a side of counselling.

At about eleven a.m. my phone rang—the phone call that knocked the calm for six.

It was my surgeon. 'Peta-Ann, you have pre-invasive breast cancer. We found a five-centimetre tumour in your milk duct. It hasn't shown up on any of the tests we've done to date. I will email you all this information and my recommendations, including single mastectomy and possibly radiation, and you should come in and see me on Wednesday so we can work through the options.'

And as the crow said: farrrrkkkkk.

I have cancer. Albeit pre-invasive, but I have cancer. Yes, the size of my breasts stifled their attempts to kill me. Their superhero status has outwitted their own evilness. But still, I have cancer. And as I had been saying for the past month, *If it is, it is, and I'll just deal with it.* That was the 'it is' moment, and the moment I entered pragmatic 'deal with it' mode.

Managing communication: you, me, them, us

At some point in our lives, we've all learnt a wee bit about grief counselling, and we've all read the associated 'how to survive' memes on that scientifically factual source of information, the Book of Face. I'm a communicator by trade, but this one stumped me. How do you tell folks you have just been diagnosed with cancer?

I was definitely in a fortunate position, as I already practiced Reiki, mindfulness and meditation at the time of my diagnosis. Having been clinically diagnosed with PTSD some years prior to my breast cancer diagnosis, I was grateful to know what an emotional toolbox was at this stage too, but could I implement any of the things I'd been taught? Well, no, I couldn't. There was simply too much going on from a medical point of view, let alone what was going on at a personal level. And for me, PTSD adds an additional level of emotional shutdown for survival.

There you are: just been diagnosed and dropped unceremoniously into a highly medicalised world. Moreover, I was faced with having to tell people what was going on, as well as being faced with my emotions and responses along with *their* emotions and responses. And while I am a firm believer in individual ownership of emotions and responses, and no one has the power to make me feel anything, and vice versa, all of this was, and is, incredibly overwhelming.

As with anything, what you want to share and when you want to share information is a choice, and I certainly made some missteps in my communication choices. So many scenarios ran through my over-stimulated brain. I certainly wasn't prepared for the curveballs that came my way.

What I discovered outside of the medical arena was, like with most things in society, many of the questions or conversations lead with physical attributes such as missing cleavage, weight loss and, for me, why I hadn't lost my hair, and I was looking 'too good' to be going through cancer treatment. Yes. This was actually said to me. Unpacking it now, I do realise it was a compliment. Sadly for me, though, it's one of those unrequested opinions, based on what society determines you should look like while undergoing cancer treatment, and if you don't match the media-portrayed, headline-grabbing imagery, then you can't have *the cancer.*

Right from the offset, I found myself running the gauntlet of what is portrayed in the standard media about what you should look like after being diagnosed and undertaking treatment for breast cancer. It was very rare for me to be asked about how I was feeling, or about the life choices I was making. I understand why folks close to me don't ask me how I am feeling. I am an intuitive empath and a thinker, so asking me how I feel about something is not helpful. However, for folks who aren't as *au fait* with the ways of P-A, then I question the focus on the physical attributes of treatment. And by questioning the focus, I was able to find ways to rebel. There is always a positive to be found in every situation—you simply have to look and be open.

If I can share any learnings in the managing-communication space, it is to simply know your values, stand by them and have a list of answers prepared like you would if you were prepping for an interview. And, once again, if you don't know what your personal values are, take the time to discover them, if only for the ease it makes prepping answers to the raft of questions, especially in the early stages of diagnosis and treatment.

And finally, the best advice I can give anyone: honour yourself and do what is best for you! I discovered very early on that I didn't have the empathy or energy to manage other people's emotions. But it did take a few false starts to come to this conclusion. I'll run you through some of my classic missteps.

Straight after the phone call from my surgeon, with my pragmatic, crisis-communicator's cap on, I started contacting folks. Now, I knew I couldn't physically verbalise what was going on, so I proceeded to text folks who needed to know, or who I thought needed to know at the time. I simply couldn't face the actual conversation.

Even now it's not an easy conversation to have. There are still many folks who think I have been on extended leave or got a new job or simply just dropped out of society. And this is completely fine.

Prior to returning to work after two years on sick leave, I worked with my psychiatrist to develop strategies to address the barrage of questions which may have been thrown at me. I truly did look at it like practising for a job interview, or a situation where you need to breathe and find your words. This work gave me the ability to answer questions about where I had been with relative ease; however, changes to my physical appearance remained one of my main stumbling blocks. It's not that I'm anti-people-asking-questions—I am a journalist by trade—it's more people's lack of listening, or recognising when not to ask, or when to stop asking.

Here's a tip: if I don't respond the way you feel I should, then it is really your issue, not mine. For example, I ran into one of my former colleagues on campus on my second shift back, and, while excited to see me, they were more excited about my weight loss. Questions were asked and benign answers were given, such as, 'I've been off for a couple of years working through a health problem.' Although my tone was a definite 'please do not ask for details' in all my answers, it fell on deaf ears. I finally broke after they made the following statement to me: 'No, seriously, tell me your weight loss secret.' Many people who know me well will agree I'm not good at feeling invisible in a conversation, let alone with someone fixated on weight loss, and my answer reflects this. I simply stated, 'Cancer, but I seriously wouldn't recommend it.'

Yes, the conversation ended. No, my former colleague didn't ask any further questions. My mission had been accomplished, albeit in a rather direct manner, but this incident once again reminded me that from the day I was diagnosed, the communication challenge kicked in.

You spend so much time and energy running the gauntlet of people not knowing what to say to you that you feel invisible in conversations, and the big one for me, which I hadn't ever considered until the day I was diagnosed, was how others need to communicate how they feel about what's happening to you.

What you want to share and when you want to share information is a choice and I certainly made some missteps in my communication choices.

This was incredibly challenging for me as an independent, high-functioning person. It didn't occur to me that I would need to take on board how others may react to my news. *Me. It's happening to me.* It simply didn't occur to me that folks cared and would be devastated by what was happening to me. And perhaps that is an insight about the level of self-worth and self-love I had at the time.

My younger brother was hilarious—after the initial shock, that is. And when I finally had the 'd'oh!' moment and sucked up the grief choking my words and called him, after the moments of disbelief and discussing the mastectomy with immediate reconstruction option my surgeon had mentioned, he simply said—and to this day I am forever grateful for this statement — 'Now you can shop in designer lingerie stores for things other than perfume.' Yes, our clan is really good at using humour to deflect. It's certainly a useful trait to have inherited.

Back to the text I had sent as my way of traversing the challenge of communicating when I wasn't able to verbalise. A number of phone calls in response to my text ensued. Apparently, it didn't occur to folks there was an actual reason I had sent a text as opposed to calling.

One of the most insensitive and egoic came from a member of my work team: 'I don't sense that it's fatal. In fact, I don't sense there's anything wrong. Are they sure they're right?' Please know, this is not an appropriate response, and also not the worst response I had to deal with. However, it is truly an indication of what not to say to someone who has just been diagnosed. And yes, once again, I recognise this is more about their issues than my actual diagnosis, but please remember *reflection*—if someone sends you a text with their devastating news about themselves, put that person at the forefront, even just briefly, and take on board that they have chosen to send you a message for a reason, and respect this.

Another strange occurrence is that you are suddenly faced with folks whom you feel will be fabulously supportive but are not, and ones who truly are fabulous but you wouldn't have even considered being so. One of my colleagues in particular was simply elegantly beautiful in his response. I didn't expect him to respond at all. I'm not even sure why I sent him the message in the first place—there's that intuition sneaking in once again. But when he called me, I knew he was genuinely concerned and sad. I could finally breathe in an actual conversation. To this day I'm not sure he realises exactly how grateful I was and am for this.

Telling immediate family members was challenging for me too. However, it was another opportunity for me to realise that your life does matter to other people, and one really needs to take notice of this and be incredibly grateful for the love of family and friends, no matter how frustrating you may find it on occasion.

And then there's the ongoing medical conversations and communication challenges you need to be prepared for. Being the introvert that I am, I choose to attend medical appointments alone. If you are like me, I highly recommend making sure you take notes, or at least allow your doctor or specialist to write notes for you. And if someone does come with you, they are your designated note-taker. I have a specific notebook that travels everywhere with me so I can write down any questions when they randomly pop into my head. I also had it at appointments to take notes to remind myself what was going on and what was agreed to. It sounds a bit of a pffaff, but seriously, your brain is full. The filing cabinet is so full it cannot take any more files, so note-taking becomes your saviour.

By taking notes you are also able to remind yourself of what you were thinking without putting yourself through the challenge of remembering. When your brain's filing cabinet is full and the trauma button has been pushed, remembering becomes one of the greatest challenges.

As a sidebar on the memory front, I even had to resort to placing notes on the cupboard next to the microwave to remind me the cupboard wasn't the microwave after trying to steam vegetables in it on a number of occasions. As hilarious as it is—and it truly is when one is waiting for the cupboard to go *bing*—your brain really does become incredibly overwhelmed. I cannot encourage you more to actively take notes, even if it's just so you can empty the filing cabinet just that wee bit to be able to cognitively process the next steps.

The next medical conversation was a doozy too. Three days after the diagnosis phone call, I rocked up to see my surgeon to discuss options. She hit me with the news that the clinician team—surgeons and oncologists among others—had met that morning, and my situation was one of three they discussed. They put all my films up on the big screen. No imaging had picked up the five-centimetre tumour in my milk duct, and because of this there is a high chance that it will turn up in my other breast and go undetected. They recommended a bilateral mastectomy.

In the space of three days I had gone from the challenges of having extra-large breasts to having their size potentially save me from invasive breast cancer to being told the best option for long-term survival was to have both breasts removed. Amputated. One low self-esteem extreme to the other.

But there was a glimmer of hope for 'normality': immediate reconstruction. At the same time as the mastectomy, I could have the reconstruction process commenced and be on the way to looking socially acceptable for the first time in my life. Could it really be that simple? My intuition was once again running rampant: *Arrrrhhhh . . . nope*. But why wasn't I immediately baulking at the need to fit into society? I had never wanted to fit in before this.

Looking back, you realise why. It's simple: it's the trauma of the situation. Your filing cabinet is completely full, and this is why you are taking incessant notes to be able to hold conversations. Despite this, you are being asked to make decisions with seemingly limited information. And this is not due to a lack of input or information from my surgeon, it was more from a 'when would I have ever considered I would be having this conversation?' place. How would I have known what questions I should have been asking?

I was incredibly grateful when my surgeon gave me two specific websites to access validated information from, with the added warning to not do an interweb search on breast cancer. As a trained journalist, I completely understand the unvalidated rabbit holes of hearsay and conjecture that are readily available on the interweb. I stuck to the two sites she recommended.

Did any of the information I read stick? Absolutely not. Despite being great resources, your brain is processing the trauma of diagnosis. Remembering to breathe can be challenging, let alone processing lots of new information to try to make informed decisions.

I also do not have any magical solutions for navigating this. For me, time for thinking was later. However, if you do have time, take it. Breathe and begin focusing on what you feel is the best outcome for you to live well beyond breast cancer. And then start asking your questions. Perhaps start with, 'What are all the options post-mastectomy?' Ask about aesthetically flat closure, if this is where your choices are leading you. And never fear asking for second opinions if your surgeon isn't one who performs AFC.

While I am not someone who regrets things—you are where you are always meant to be, etc.—hindsight is an interesting thing. I do wish I had the brain space to take the time to consider all options prior to my mastectomy. For me, based on the clinician's advice, my options were simple. Option A included radiation; a life of 'what if-ing'; a single mastectomy; a reduction of the right breast; becoming lopsided, out of balance; hormone therapy; and the high probability of it re-occurring in my right breast. Option B was a bilateral mastectomy, a slim chance of hormone therapy, a slim chance of radiation, and a 98 percent no-return rate. Both options included immediate reconstruction. My surgeon asked if I wanted time to consider my options before making my decision. See what I mean by 'if you have time, take it'? I personally didn't see I had any real options. Bilateral mastectomy it was. Interestingly, though, this was quite possibly the easiest decision I have ever made. And an appointment with the first reconstruction and aesthetic surgeon was made.

And wasn't that intriguing an appointment. For those who may not be aware, a reconstruction and aesthetic surgeon is essentially a very qualified cosmetic surgeon—no disrespect intended. It hadn't even been a week since I'd received the news that I actually had early-stage breast cancer, and I was being told by the next specialist, 'No, you can't have immediate reconstruction due to the size of your breasts, and you'll have to lose weight so my work is aesthetically pleasing.' *Arrrhhhhh! I've just been diagnosed with cancer; not sure I care about being aesthetically pleasing right now.*

More tears. I had been holding it together really well with the prospect of immediate reconstruction, and that was taken away from me in the space of twenty minutes. Three more rounds of surgery awaited me post-mastectomy, to achieve what society may classify as 'normal' in breast size, thus deeming me socially acceptable.

Once again, the societal norm of women equals breasts was smacking me in the face. Not only was I in a consultation discussing having my breasts rebuilt so I could feel normal again, but the discussion also included the pearlers of being 'more normal-sized', as they couldn't reconstruct breasts as big as mine. Interestingly, at no point in any discussion was I asked what it would take for me to feel normal after having a mastectomy.

Ever the thinker and analyst, my communication-advisor brain kicks in every now and then, and this scenario highlighted a communication gap . . . I know, right?

My breast surgeon was doing everything possible to keep my spirits up, and working with an unusually pragmatic and humour-deflecting patient is quite challenging, I can tell you. And then you arrive at the next specialist and they're like, 'Arh, nope, scientifically not possible.'

Hope fades quickly of 'normality' returning, and all because of different communication styles.

It's an interesting dichotomy. On one hand you are navigating the emotions and response of those close to you and attempting to communicate as effectively as possible while remaining as detached as possible. And on the other, you have some specialists who seemingly forget there is an actual person with feelings and emotions attached to the breasts being discussed.

A recent couple of clangers for me were a random clinician referring to mastectomy scarring and rolled ribs as a 'deformity', and being told on several occasions I 'only' had pre-invasive breast cancer.

Oddly, the 'only' is the most interesting for me. As said to me often by my treatment team, did folks want me to hang around and wait until it was invasive stage 4 before I started treatment? Would I have had to have a total hysterectomy and oophorectomy, after polyps were discovered, to prevent endometrial and ovarian cancer, throwing me into the surgically induced menopause deep end, if it was 'only'?

Word choices are so vital at any stage of treatment and recovery, and, well, life in general.

Don't get me wrong. These standouts have been occasional anomalies throughout my odyssey. I truly have been blessed with my treatment team and their ability to understand my communication style and needs. My team is full of specialists who know and remember I am a real person, and if a new one is recommended and they do not understand my style or energy, then they don't get accepted as part of my treatment team. This is another way I have achieved doing what's best for me and following my intuition.

I left the reconstruction surgeon's rooms visibly upset. I wasn't really sure what I had just agreed to other than I was having a bilateral mastectomy which didn't include immediate reconstruction. Suddenly my surgery date was scheduled, and treatment really commenced. Absolutely no going back. Here's where one life ends and a new one begins.

So, here we go. It's July 15, 2015. The tune playing on the radio on the way to the hospital is 'All About That Bass' by Meghan Trainor—pretty poignant when you're about to undergo a bilateral mastectomy. My surgeon and breast-care nurse and a team of anaesthetists were hanging with me in pre-op. Did I mention I am super challenging when it comes to anaesthetic? No? Well, just to make the specialist's life a little more interesting, your standard general anaesthetic has the propensity to cause me and some of my family members to shuffle off this mortal coil. In fact, one already has. So I always end up with the larger-than-average anaesthetist team and plethora of medical folks watching me.

Back to the July 15 pre-op procedure. Another thing I am forever grateful of is my surgeon's acceptance of my communication style. It is based in humour and detached from emotion. This occurs for a number of reasons, but this is me. We were in pre-op and my surgeon asked the standard question: 'What are we doing today?' My response: 'You're cutting my tits off.' Her response: 'And what else are we doing?' I responded in my best ABC radio voice: 'You are undertaking a sentinel node biopsy after performing a bilateral mastectomy.' She smiled. The rest of the team were standing there, mouths and jaws on the floor, stunned at the exchange with 'did she really just say that' looks on their faces. They'd only just met me. But I can guarantee my surgeon was grateful for this exchange. She knew in an instant I was as okeh as I could be going into this life-altering surgery, simply by understanding my communication style.

As for the rest of the day: bilateral mastectomy, sentinel node biopsy, six kilograms lighter in three hours. Four drains. Two scars which would turn into four, and a wound from one arm hole to the other after more surgery a few months later. The surgeon requiring physio due to the enormousness of my breasts. Tumour-free, for now. Looking forward to living life well, beyond breast cancer.

However, now the real fun begins: when the fine print kicks in . . .

Am I a woman now?

I discovered very early in my recovery that the concept of feeling normal, or like a woman, after having a bilateral mastectomy takes on a life of its own. There are so many decision points which constitute defining 'normal' to make while you are attempting to simply survive the enormity of what has occurred and ultimately thrive beyond treatment.

And then there's all the incredibly well-meaning folks who are struggling with how they feel about what has happened to you, and they want everything to go 'back to normal' as well. They want you to be who you were. They want you to look like you did. They want you to feel like a woman again. But once again, they forget to ask you what this means for you and if indeed you are no longer 'feeling like a woman'.

What did it mean for me? I can guarantee that, while in the throes of the initial treatment phase, this was a very difficult question to answer.

Acceptance and being at one with your new world are all over there in the distance as you navigate all the things that are happening to your mind, body and soul in the present moment, let alone understanding whether or not you really want to be what society determines to be normal, or a new version of it.

I did not wish to conform. However, I was yet to remember my longstanding rebellious 'celebrate your uniqueness' mindset. And sadly, everything that is going on around you and with you has a distinct emphasis on looking backwards and being like you were before, before your world became incredibly different and yet more authentically you . . . if people dare to ask you what being normal is for you, that is.

I was quickly realising, well before I'd concretely made my decision regarding staying flat permanently, that a big part of this looking backwards by all and sundry was their way of coping and another 'save the boobs' thought process. Another 'being a normal woman means you must have breasts' moment. It was simply presumed that this is what I wanted. Why would anyone choose a different route? And from what I have experienced since, this is a presumption made on behalf of all mastectomy recipients.

But I wonder how many of us are actually asked at any point if this concept of normal resonates with us. I certainly wasn't.

For me, this is a disrespectful approach as well. Minimising or not seeking someone else's thoughts and feelings out of some misguided intention to ensure they fit in is disrespectful towards the person who is living through the trauma. A life decision is being determined with little or no input from the person on the receiving end of the decision.

This is up there with the use of the term 'holding space' in complementary therapy circles in my world. It is a beautiful intention to be unconditionally supportive of someone going through trauma. However, did you ask the person if this is what they needed or wanted, or is it your assumption of what the person requires? The misguided determination of 'holding space' for someone without actually asking them is disrespectful, and akin to all the decision points in seeking the 'normal' holy grail after a bilateral mastectomy. Ask the person what they feel, think and may want. It truly is that simple.

Yes, all the treatment and decision points are overwhelming; however, this doesn't mean we cannot be asked what we think or feel is best for our long-term future. It may take a wee bit longer to figure it out, but here's a top tip: never presume you know how someone else will respond or that they will think the same way as you.

Unless you experience the exact same circumstances at the exact same age, etc., this will never be possible. So instead of presuming you know what your partner, friend, daughter, cousin, etc. needs to feel like a woman, stop. Think. Then ask.

I'm quite well known for being a thinker, so it still baffles me when folk don't ask me the obvious questions. It is a simple question: 'Did having a mastectomy cause you to feel any less of a woman?'

I have a different answer now to what I would have potentially said while I was still processing whether I wanted reconstruction or not. But I tell you what, I would have been so grateful for being asked the question instead of the presumption. Or for others wishing I could be the person I once was.

I shall share some interesting ways not asking the obvious question manifested in my world, real-life scenarios to provide some idea of what I am referring to. While not the only examples I could share, they are the most poignant and happened only months after my bilateral. I am also truly grateful for these incidents, as they too played an integral role in defining what I felt was normal for me, leading me to celebrate my uniqueness.

Here goes. At first, I was taken aback. Vaguely insulted. Definitely perplexed. Looking for the kindness in the statement posed. I knew there was kindness there, I just had to keep looking for it. The folks doing the proposing wouldn't be saying this without some level of kindness and compassion, surely? Even though it was incredibly misguided. And what of this statement? Simple, really: 'Let me know if you need me to make you feel like a woman again. I'd be more than happy to assist.' Wow. Now do you see why I was mildly perplexed?

And wait for it . . . not one but two gentlemen made this offer. Nope, they did not know each other, so no conferring. These were genuinely independent offers, within days of each other. Perhaps I was portraying the 'hey, how you doin?' vibe a little too strongly (this is me definitely being sarcastic. And to continue the sarcasm, such a vibe is to be expected only a couple of months after being diagnosed with breast cancer and having a bilateral mastectomy, and while also dealing with becoming very suddenly single just prior to diagnosis).

I do hope folks are catching on that I declined both offers, and on all occasions, as apparently saying no once didn't confirm my lack of desire for such a misplaced offer.

I could analyse the motivation for the offers and go into all manner of niceties and reasons for their collective offers—ya know: 'that's how they were processing my situation', 'they didn't know what to say or do', 'I'm normally their support team not the person needing the support', 'their way to buoy my self-esteem', etc. But here's the thing: their wayward offers had the completely opposite effect.

Suddenly, I was confronted with (and way too early in my recovery I might add) *Is this going to be my life now?* And from a relationship point of view, *Only good enough to be the bit on the side, or freak-show status?* And I know the gents involved well enough to know they truly would be mortified to think their offer sparked such thoughts. But here's the thing, lads: it did. To be fair, I have shared this with both of them, but I am still not convinced they understand.

And this is when I started to do what I do best: ponder.

Why is society so focused on looks and sexuality? And why is breast cancer awareness so sexualised? The example I raised earlier—when during my first Pink October post-surgery I was so excited to see a local tradies ute all decked out in pink and breast cancer awareness symbols until I saw the added slogan across the back windscreen: save the boobs—says it all, really.

These are rhetorical questions, by the way. I wouldn't be pondering this if I hadn't been conditioned somewhat by society's focus on 'pretty' or 'sexy' or my most despised word of all: 'hot'. And anyone who knows me knows I buck the system in any way I can, purely because I have never fit the stereotypical society-conditioned mould of 'hot' or 'pretty'. And yet I am very aware that I possess elegance, grace, style, presence, inner light and beauty, both when I was at my most buxom wenchiness and now at my bawdy (play on words, people—flat as a board now) wenchiness.

The statement which perplexed me most was about regaining that 'womanly feeling'. Like somehow having the 'girls amputated' to save my life meant I was no longer a woman. It truly hadn't occurred to me that I was no longer a woman until I was offered 'servicing', so to speak.

What had occurred to me was I had spent most of my life battling self-esteem issues stemming from my super-sized breasts. They weighed almost 6 kg. I would relish anyone who spoke to my face as opposed to the girls. I knew they were distracting—I lived with them. I also knew how to use their charms. But seriously, I didn't like them one bit. And yet I allowed myself and my worth to be defined by them. Towards the end of their life, I truly felt completely defined by their enormous presence.

Needless to say, I was astonished to find that once they were gone I was still being defined by them, transforming from pinup girl, so to speak, to apparently no longer being a woman.

So what did I learn from these incidents? Simple, really. It reminded me that, although I don't realise it most days, I do actually stand up for my values and even my self-worth, my self-respect and, dare I say it, self-love. It reminded me that I am worthy of a loving, kind, equal partnership, and I don't have to accept being a societal reject simply because I do not conform to the norm. It also reminded me that I simply do not have to accept what is thrown at me and be content with whatever romantic attention comes my way. I had never accepted this previously, so why should I start accepting it now?

Most days I even forget that I'm no longer 'normal'. Since my mastectomy and my decision to stay flat—flat and fabulous, in fact—I have learnt many ways to minimise my apparent appearance of 'not normal'. I achieve this through the use of colour and rocking my own personal style, as well as working on my mind, soul and spirit. I am blown away daily by the fact that folks don't even notice I no longer have breasts.

On the odd occasion, my PTSD kicks in and I suddenly feel as though everyone is noticing the rolled-under rib cage where my breasts used to reside. But after a wee bit of processing, I am now able to recognise the difference between people actually noticing and my flight response kicking in, and I have a number of well-being tactics in my Elegantly Unique Toolkit (my version of the emotional toolkit) to get through these moments. I shall go into more detail about my toolkit a wee bit later, however, just so you know what sort of toolkit I mean, mine has things like meditation, movement, writing and some other woo-woo things in it to get me through.

What I can also share and recommend is: follow your intuition about the attention you are receiving, good or bad. I think folks forget that what we have been through is horrendous and traumatic. It's not akin to having your appendix out, as it is often explained in medical pamphlets due to a mastectomy being referred to medically as 'non-invasive surgery'. And we are certainly not the latest act at the local circus. We deserve the same, if not more, respect and tenderness than we accepted in our previous life.

If you find yourself in a similar situation to me, really follow your intuition. Your heart and soul are more than likely telling your head what truly is going on before your head actually catches up with the situation.

If your intuition radar is going off about someone, call them on it. No one ever said you weren't a kind, generous, gracious soul for standing up for yourself and what feels right for you—not the other person, just you.

Also, be authentic. Your breasts don't define you. Your lack of breasts doesn't define you. None of this defines whether you feel like a woman or not. Society doesn't get to tell you this. That's the job of your authentic, beautiful soul.

Above all, stick to your values and never allow anyone to dim the light that shines around your beliefs. I firmly believe in kindness, humour, love, courage and good coffee, and if someone isn't able to join me in my beliefs, see ya! And this certainly doesn't lessen my value as a woman.

Maybe they can grow back after all

Early in my recovery, I was catching up with a friend who had been diagnosed around the same time as me. Her treatment plan was lumpectomy and chemo. She was rocking a gorgeous head scarf this particular day we caught up for coffee. During our conversation, I made the simple statement I was really looking forward to my first haircut in absolute months, since before my mastectomy, in fact. She just looked at me. And before I could blurt out an apology for my misguided statement, she said the following: 'At least my hair grows back.' Simple as that. *Touché*.

Her witty retort got me thinking: *Maybe breasts can magically grow back after being amputated?*

Growing up I believed my paternal grandmother had superpowers. How did I come to this conclusion? One of her front teeth was dark grey and no longer a living tooth. Why? Put simply, it was her third front tooth. Her adult front tooth was knocked out playing basketball or something and a third one grew in its place.

My body also seemed to have inherited some of her special growing powers. As a child I had my adenoids removed three times. Yup. They're not meant to grow back after being removed the first time, let alone the second.

Magical superpowers. I sensed a theme developing . . . maybe my girls could magically grow back too, albeit with some surgical assistance. After all, they have already shown their superpowers over their life—and then came the reality smackdown.

We've all heard of the evil, evil, evil Body Mass Index (BMI); you know, the one that was invented to measure epidermis by an insurance company using males only as the test group, and somehow morphed into how many members of the medical profession determine if we are underweight, normal, overweight, significantly overweight, excessively overweight or obese.

This system is based on the height-weight ratio only. There is no consideration for muscle composition, bone structure, basal metabolic rate, etc. In fact, a bodybuilder with zero body fat generally falls into the obese category of the BMI scale.

And while I recognise that medically there currently isn't a better way to measure one's body mass, and just in case it's not coming through in this, I am soooo not a fan of the BMI. But wait. What on earth has BMI got to do with breast cancer recovery, embracing my uniqueness and whether or not the girls will grow back, I hear you ask? Plenty.

Within months of undergoing my bilateral mastectomy, BMI became everything in my world. In fact, it became my cancer deflection. My life morphed from recovering from breast cancer and preventing metastaticisation to achieving an imaginary BMI number.

It may surprise you to know that, on top of the trauma of being diagnosed with cancer, increasingly mastectomy ladies are being informed that reconstruction cannot be undertaken until their BMI is below 30. Please know, there are incredibly sound medical and scientific reasons for the weight loss. Reconstruction surgery alone can be up to a twelve-hour event, so you certainly need to be at the optimal version of you, health-wise, to simply endure this surgery. However, why is there reliance on BMI to determine this? How many folks do you know who are healthy—and I emphasise *clinically healthy*, not the media-determined version of healthy—and have the correct BMI classification?

I am aware of the number of scientific and medical studies linking weight to breast cancer. In fact, in the early 1990s, while working at Fairfax Media, I was researching a piece on breast cancer and discovered that a Swedish study connected women over 175 cm tall and overweight to being more susceptible to breast cancer. More foretelling—what hope did I have, at 178 cm tall and obese according to BMI?

Back to reality. In early September 2015, a couple of months after having the girls amputated—in fact, prior to being fitted for prosthesis—my breast care nurse (BCN) had to make an awful phone call to me. Well, another one.

After my disastrous meeting with the first plastic surgeon around immediate reconstruction, we had made some enquiries to see if I could have reconstruction as an intermediate in the public system.

A small digression: despite being diagnosed with breast cancer and having a bilateral mastectomy as a part of treatment, reconstruction is classified as elective cosmetic surgery. I kid you not. And even with the highest hospital cover, private health insurance reconstruction costs can be well over $15k. At this stage, with my savings being eaten away by treatment costs and not earning what I once did, I was incredibly grateful for any potential financial assistance in achieving the allegedly 'normal' goal.

But what of the phone call—as I channel *The Rocky Horror Picture Show* again, cueing the foreboding music and dark, stormy haunted house—there was a possibility to go intermediate; however, the new plastic surgeon saw on a piece of paper (with no physical consultation with me) my height and weight, and deemed that I had to decrease my BMI by at least eight points before they would undertake the surgery.

Suddenly, to regain control of my world and regain some sense of normality, according to society, I had to lose a gazillion kilos. See the irony here? I certainly didn't, for months! And my poor, poor, poor BCN! She had inadvertently discovered my lifelong Achilles heel: BMI and fitting a preconceived mould of 'normal' weight makes . . . my . . . blood . . . boil. Still. There were tears. Lots and lots of tears. Finally, some would say.

Please don't misunderstand. Yes, I was carrying extra kilos. Yes, I needed to lose weight as part of cancer prevention. But going from your diagnosis of a bilateral with immediate reconstruction, which got knocked on the head two days after my diagnosis due to the immenseness of the girls to another 'nope, no reconstruction until you lose a trillion +1 kilos, cos on paper your BMI is way too high', is simply soul-destroying. And classically, the surgeon asking my BCN to pass on this info did not offer any how-to's.

In a world where I was working so hard to find my new authentic self, I was once again being asked to change. Will I ever be enough? However, change is a choice and one only you can make. It's irrelevant how many folks tell you to or request you to, it's your choice. But once again I found myself handing over my personal power and following the normal path. All of this angst and the roadblocks to achieve this mythical 'normal' feeling after a bilateral mastectomy . . . why wasn't I following my inner knowing as I would 'normally' do?

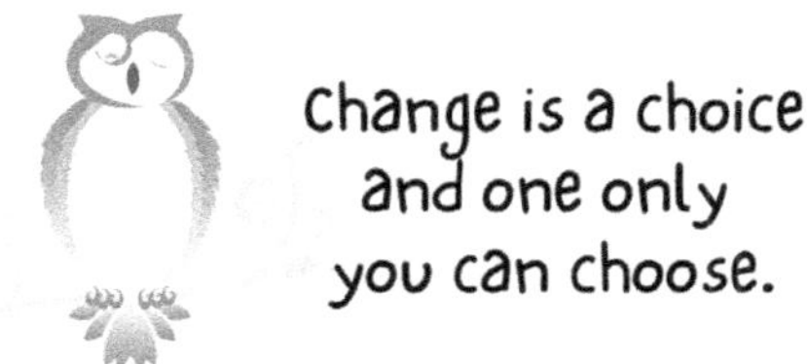

So, after the tears, the fuming, and a wee bit of classic ten-year-old Peta-Ann foot-stamping tantrum, I followed my heart and my gut and suddenly remembered to be my authentic self. My world is about choices, and this was my choice. The only person who could come up with a plan was me.

From a physicality point of view, not only does having a bilateral affect one's ability to exercise—especially when your upper-body strength magically disappears with your breasts and the scar tissue limits your movement, and then there's the popping ribs and the falling over as your body realigns your gait—I was also contending with dodgy limbs from a violent car crash years ago. My knees didn't bend, etc., and my previous orthopaedic surgeon had banned me from all impactful exercise, meaning I was allowed to do water-based exercise only.

My BCN sourced as many non-surgical ideas as possible: hydrotherapy and a nurse practitioner who specialised in weight management. I went into solution mode and approached my naturopath and oncology physio for assistance.

My naturopath and I re-jigged my diet slightly to be more alkaline—also perfect for cancer prevention. I was already dairy- and gluten-free, so out went all starches and sugars, in particular fructose, legumes, grains and other stuff. We added a few superfoods, such as cinnamon, cacao, ginger and cardamom to my daily concoctions, and most importantly worked on actually eating. Yes, I was—and still am, if I am brutally honest—one of those folks who chose not to eat, which morphed into forgetting to eat as I no longer got hungry. I do believe it will always be my default position; however, every day I actively choose to eat healthy.

My oncology physiotherapist was another revelation to me. At the time, her practice was based on cancer rehab. This included oncology physio, pain management, lymphatic massage, counselling, a dietician and a newly appointed exercise physiologist. Guess who her first client was? Correct. 'Twas moi. Sadly, at no point in sourcing assistance did I put two and two together and come up with four—four being 'this is not about replacement girls or fitting into society's version of normal, this is about living from now on as my new me'. Thriving beyond breast cancer. Celebrating my uniqueness. Being authentic and stylish and the best version of myself despite all the change thrown my way.

Add in the nurse practitioner my BCN sourced, my psychiatrist, my meditation group and my own Reiki treatment, and I had all bases covered, from food, exercise, counselling, and soul nourishment to sleep hygiene. Yup, *hygiene*—an odd word, but that's what they call it, and it is very relevant to weight loss as well as breast cancer.

With my team gathered, my weight-loss journey commenced towards reconstruction, as my breasts had strangely chosen to not grow back as yet. And I still continued to miss the point about what was best for me. And still no one had asked me what I felt was the best version of normal for me.

I was completely devastated, of course, that I had not dropped 10 kg in the first three weeks. Me and my personal expectations. I had lost 3.5 kg, which was apparently fabulous! However, within three months I'd dropped 17 kg. And this is when the penny started its drop. By the way, have I mentioned previously how much I despise the word 'journey' these days? I simply do. And I am not alone among those of us who have been diagnosed either. But as there is no better word to describe events, sometimes I will grin and bear it. I prefer 'odyssey'.

My weight loss was on schedule to achieve the elusive BMI required by the plastic surgeon in early 2016. However, I had not had an appointment with the new reconstruction surgeon as yet. My only reconstruction consult was a couple of days after my diagnosis, and all I can recall is them taking an emergency phone call while they examined my breasts and talking about what work they would need to do, and they left me standing half naked while they took said phone call during my consultation. Hmm . . . so it really wasn't the optimal time to be asking questions about process, etc.

Me being the thinker that I am—and I am positive most folks in this situation would be doing the same thing—I thought, *What on earth does reconstruction entail?* I knew that, even I could afford it, I couldn't have the trans-flap version, as I have a massive appendectomy scar. 'Trans-flap' is where they take live tissue from an area such as your abdomen and reconstruct your breasts with it. It is truly amazing surgery, as they reconnect all the little veins so your rebuilt breasts are alive, so to speak. But with my appendix scar, there was limited live tissue in the area needed.

I was looking at the expanders-and-implants version of reconstruction that was available at the time, and I had a myriad of questions. I began asking members of Team P-A Weight Loss, and my fabulous physio once again pointed me in the correct direction.

In 2016 there was a general lack of information provided to Australian women on post-mastectomy reconstruction. My physio had a solution. Enter stage right: a great group affiliated with the Breast Cancer Network Australia (BCNA) called 'Reclaim Your Curves', where us BC chicks can ask questions and discuss issues openly and candidly with other BC mastectomy chicks. Excellent. So I joined and requested a chat with the Queensland ambassador. Another gorgeous lady. And this is when the penny finally dropped.

During the chat with the then beautiful ambassador, she used the phrase, 'I just wanted to feel normal' repeatedly when sharing her story about treatment and reconstruction.

Normal. It's an interesting term. As I've mentioned, it's not a word that resonates with me. And it would appear I will continue this trait. During the conversation, so much was shared and discussed about how it's becoming increasingly *normal* to go through what we go through: diagnosis, surgery, treatment and reconstruction—although reconstruction was not automatically part of the whole odyssey, unlike the United Kingdom or United States of America, where, at the time, reconstruction was automatically part of a mastectomy treatment plan. And on top of the lack of information available, when it comes to reconstruction the weight-loss curveball is thrown at us. Medically, I get it. Truly. But we're people in a fragile state, so for some—like me, initially—reconstruction is the light at the end of the tunnel. When the goalposts get moved consistently, it has a detrimental effect. So much change. So much expected of us, which we have to process. So much to work out, so we can feel truly at peace with ourselves. So much to work through to discover how to be our new selves and truly authentic.

After our chat, I sat for a while watching the ocean—I was blessed to live on the shoreline at this time in my life—and it dawned on me: I truly don't feel abnormal without breasts. This was my 'stylish and authentic' moment, celebrating my unique self. I was not simply putting on a brave face, I truly felt my version of normal is without breasts. Simple as that. I had finally started to join all the dots together.

My pondering mode continued down a meltdown path, of course. *What does this all mean? Am I completely mad for even contemplating staying flat?*

I made an appointment to see my BCN to discuss not having reconstruction and staying flat. Hilariously, while my BCN knew I'd been losing weight and was keeping the reconstruction surgeon who requested the dramatic weight loss up to date on my progress, she had not seen me since she pulled the last of my four drains out. She did not recognise me in the hall outside day oncology. Her jaw dropped, literally. And I was only 17 kg lighter at that point.

So we met and chatted. And it was during this chat that the penny clanged loudly in my head: *This isn't about losing weight for a reconstruction surgeon. This is about living my life, uniquely, stylishly and authentically, for me and how I want it to be.*

Turns out, my BCN was unsurprised by my revelation that I was leaning towards not having reconstruction and choosing to spend my life flat and fabulous. Apparently, her larger-breasted ladies relished in the sense of freedom—her term was 'liberation'—that no longer having breasty dumplings brings. I agree completely. Although it is not without issue, clearly. I am a conundrum, though—of course I am. Apparently, it's rather uncommon for her ladies to feel more conspicuous wearing prostheses than not wearing them. I really feel incredibly fake wearing them, and feel like everyone else senses the inauthenticity. That's my version of reality, folks. More about the role this plays in a bit.

And as for that penny clanging inside my head, well, it was an interesting tune indeed. 'Normal' for me is about being stylish and authentic, to celebrate my uniqueness and be the best version of me I can be. Breasts simply don't grow back naturally, despite my childhood thoughts that us Wood's are incredibly special, magical folks. We are, but apparently there is a limit to our magical powers!

For me to be the authentic person I need to be, reconstruction is not an option either.

What a revelation, and all inside my head while attempting to have a coherent conversation with my BCN. The seed was planted. My authentic new me was heading down the path of no return and no reconstruction.

But what of the gazillion and one kilograms I was meant to be losing to achieve that illusive BMI for the reconstruction surgeon? Simple, really. I finally heard my inner self chatting away and I have chosen to release my weight for me, my ongoing wellbeing, and as part of my cancer prevention regimen, not for anyone else.

Weight management will always be a part of my uniqueness. It's been a lifelong journey and aspiration, quite literally. Since birth, even. And my epigenetic coding is to protect and guard. So while I'm protecting and guarding, I will always be shy of society's version of normal—weight-wise on top of everything else. And if I am strong and healthy, I'm more than happy to celebrate this uniqueness instead of striving for an unobtainable version of normal.

By the way, I still follow my alkaline diet as part of my prevention regimen, thanks to my naturopath. Buuuut . . . I do eat chocolate and other forms of deliciousness. How? Cos I make it! There may even be a few of my recipes at the end of this book. Have a gander and enjoy.

Ribs bellies and physics

Personally, the title of this chapter sounds more like getting ready for a giant barbeque, but it is quite a serious discussion.

My no-reconstruction decision has all but been cemented firmly in my brain . . . well, almost. And now my brain has the capacity to focus on the fine print about bilateral mastectomy consequences, the stuff you are never going to know or understand unless you are actually living it. And it would be seriously wrong if anyone expected others to understand as well. This is the stuff that occurs to your body and yours only after a bilateral.

There truly is only so much information the clinicians and breast care nurses can share with their clients. We are all unique, and I truly do believe if they were to share every single possible outcome currently known, it would be information overload and no one would be able to make a definitive decision about anything.

This information falls into the 'stuff no one really tells you about' category. I can guarantee, however, that none of it would have changed my decision to go through with the bilateral. That was the wisest choice I could have made to ensure I get to hang around and annoy folks just that little bit longer.

I find the fine print truly amazing, particularly from a physiological point of view. Yes, the science nerd part of my brain gets super excited about it all, despite having to live with it.

Everyone is truly different in the way their mind, body and soul respond to trauma. And I am truly grateful that medical cohorts recognise that everyone's version of breast cancer and the treatment, recovery and prevention is an individual process.

Let's start with the physical side of the fine print. Who'd have thought having a bilateral would cause such mirthful moments as popping ribs, loss of upper-body strength, falling over while trying to walk, blisters in new places on one's feet, realignment of posture, gait and arm movement changes, abdominal and arm swelling, cording—and the list goes on.

If you stop and think about it, after three rounds of surgery within six months, plus gall bladder surgery twelve months prior to my bilateral, I personally have eleven areas of scar tissue between my waist and décolletage, including a scar directly over my sternum, which turns out to be one of the most curious in the role it plays overall.

Thankfully, I have an amazing physical therapy team who were able to allay my 'am I going completely mad?' moments. But just in case you or your loved one don't have the same amazingness available to you, I hope sharing my lived experience of the fine print may assist you navigating your version in some small way.

Let's start with the ribs. As it turns out, this is a consequence that I am blessed with. Did you know that your ribs can become completely unhappy after a bilateral? I didn't, but I do now.

How did I discover this? Another great question you pose. I was at one of my plethora of appointments, the last of the week. It was a Friday. I was feeling really unwell, but not unwell as in flu unwellness, just really uncomfortable in the torso area, not able to breathe well and generally blah. I didn't have a temperature, so I knew that I wasn't lurgied-up. But I was getting to that unbearable grumpy point. This continued over the weekend. No reprieve whatsoever. Sleep had once again become optional. No eating. Sitting, standing and walking were all annoyingly painful. Monday morning rocks up and I have an appointment with my fabulous oncology physio, and I am contemplating making an appointment with my GP as well. I go to my physio appointment. Luckily for me, she is super intuitive and immediately recognises I am completely out of sorts. I explain what has been going on and she does the 'let's have a look at something' thing. Riiiight . . . and hey voila, 'P-A, this rib and that rib are anterior, and we just have to pop them back in.' So after a few Gibson-styled *Lethal Weapon* movements, some intense hugging and some odd popping noises: pain gone. Discomfort gone. Ability to breath regained. WTF?

Welcome to the world of fascia and connective tissue, and how pain in the right side of your neck can be felt in your left ankle. I know, right? I am definitely not going to go into detail as I am not an expert, but the way the body responds is absolutely fascinating.

As I mentioned previously, my breasty dumplings weighed approximately 6 kg all up. Now, if you ponder this logically, it is natural for your ribs to want to move around after they have had such a weight lifted off them.

As I also mentioned, I have eleven areas of scar tissue between my décolletage and waist, which stretches from under one arm and traverses my chest to under the other arm. And while the surgery doesn't cut muscle—hence 'non-invasive' surgery—the scar tissue and your body's instinctive protective mode has a great deal of effect on many of your muscle groups.

One breast surgeon has undertaken a study into a patient's posture pre- and post-diagnosis. Interestingly, he films—with their consent—how they walk into his rooms before receiving a cancer-positive diagnosis. In general, most people stand tall, chest open, shoulders back in a confident posture. On leaving the specialist's rooms, if they have received a 'you have breast cancer' diagnosis, the posture instantly falls into protective mood. Shoulders drop forward, chest closes up and arms are folded across the chest. Such a simple study gives so much information about the way your body responds physically to trauma, and perhaps may even provide an indication as to what form of post-treatment rehabilitation may be useful.

What I am also finding super interesting is the fact I have more shoulder issues post-mastectomy than I did pre. This is to do with scar tissue limiting upper-body movement and strength, and forever wanting to pull my shoulders forward, which leads to rotator cuff issues.

The way scar tissue interplays with your fascial muscles causes challenges throughout your body, including your pecs, chest, ribs, and thoracic spine, and the ability to grip, just for starters. All of these have obvious effects on recovery, daily tasks and returning to fulltime work. I have never broken so many pieces of crockery in my life, thanks to my loss of grip.

Twice a day every day I undertake scar-tissue-release work. Yes, I am still doing this some seven years down the track. It is going to be with me immemorially, we suspect. I am incredibly grateful to have been taught by some rather enlightened souls how to achieve this, along with muscle-isolating exercises to activate the specific muscles by body needs to turn on or off. I have become fabulous at turning on and using my lats; however, this causes issues for my pec major and pec minor, so I must turn off my lats too, on occasion.

A positive is that my posture has improved tenfold. One of the funniest things folks say to me—well, to me it's hilarious, to them it's confusing—is that I am taller. Just to let everyone know, I remain 178 cm tall. I get measured every time I have surgery, so this one I can vouch for. I *appear* taller, yes, this is true, as I am no longer slouching to hide my gargantuan breasts and, more importantly, if I don't stand up tall with shoulders dropped and rhomboids activated, I am in serious pain as a result of my bilateral. It really is that simple, people. Welcome to the new version of me. My posture is even noticed when I am out on my early-morning walk—one of the local gentlemen calls me 'proud lady'. Who knew I had it in me to walk with my chest out!

It is so interesting to me how everything is connected. You know the old nursery tune 'Your hip bone's connected to your thigh bone . . .'? Well, it is so much more than that. Working with my fabulous physical therapy team has been an eye-opener from an 'everything is definitely connected' point of view.

My ribs, pecs, scapula and rhomboids all want to protect me from more scar tissue and trauma, and I spend much cognitive energy reassuring them and ensuring they are turned-on and functioning to their optimum level to keep my pain and fatigue levels under as much control as possible. And I am not special, so to speak. I have discovered anecdotally that this is not an uncommon consequence of bilateral mastectomy.

It will perhaps take a lifetime and a lot of hard work for my body to physically find its new optimal working version. Who knows how long it will take for my scar tissue to move from resembling spaghetti to layered lasagne, if ever. It is the spaghetti similarity which is the underlying cause of the rib movement too. Basically, the scar tissue attaches to the fascial muscles which are attached to the rib-cage lining. So, if the scar tissues pulls on the fascia it pulls on the rib lining which pulls on the ribs which leads to P-A saying 'OH DEAR GAWD' loudly and often.

For me this can happen randomly and whenever it chooses. I could be doing a sideway stretch to grab something out of the pantry—not over my head, just sideways—or gardening or walking up a hill or on a rowing machine or falling over while walking and then trying to convince people it's not okeh to pull me up or falling off a park bench as it rolls over in a cyclonic gust of wind. Yes, folks, I have achieved all of these. I am particularly not a fan of the three a.m. rolling-over-in-bed version. My point is it can happen anywhere, anytime, no warning.

However, another positive is my incredible treatment team have also taught me how to use stretchy bands and ball work to release my scar tissue and manoeuvre my own ribs back into place. Yes, it's overtly uncomfortable and rather pain-inducing. And some of my ribs need another person to help me get them back into place, and depending on the magnitude of their movement, my partner has also been trained by my team to hug me just the right way too. All this training comes in handy at a moment's notice, and on occasion allows me to breathe deeply when meditating—one of my ultimate goals these days—between appointments with my amazing physio.

Despite having so much to remember and work on every day as a consequence of my bilateral mastectomy, I can honestly say I wouldn't have changed my decision to have it had I known how my body would respond, if for no other reason than I'm still here to learn all this new information about how your body functions.

The additional positive consequence of how my body has responded post-bilateral is I intuitively listen to it a wee bit better now. And while I have always sensed issues or concerns, I was not the best at taking notice of my intuition. But sometimes all roads lead to Rome, and your intuition simply becomes too in-your-face and you have to take notice. For me, the listening bit remains a work in progress.

And how does all this newfound knowledge about ribs, muscles and fascia assist me in moving forward in the most stylish and authentic way possible? How was I going to implement all this newfound knowledge on strength-training in my real life? For me it was to return to my high-functioning working life. I simply needed to earn money so I could pay the mortgage and the medical bills. So, I started contemplating going back to work. I use the word 'back' deliberately.

As a writer and communicator, my world was based around being in front of a computer or a notebook with a pen in hand—old school. And when you are in the moment, on a roll or meeting a deadline, time gets away from you. But the new version of Peta-Ann may never regain these qualities. My treatment team and I had spent a great deal of effort, time, sweat and tears (no blood, thankfully) working on whether or not I would return to my old work persona. The mind and soul fine print is screaming '*Noooooooooo!*' about now too. See aforementioned statement about my intuition being a learning curve in itself.

At the fifteen-month mark post-bilateral, as part of my 'surely I am ready to go back to work' thought process, I decided to test the waters and see how much work I could achieve from a physical point of view. I set myself some tasks, just your normal business paperwork: tax returns, research, assignment writing, and a timeframe to achieve the tasks in: five hours a day over three days, as the plan was to return to work full-time. I planned to take breaks every twenty minutes to make sure I didn't cause myself too much grief. The plan worked well on day one. And while I was incredibly exhausted mentally and physically, I was also very pleased and proud of what I had achieved.

Day two started well, but some old habits were slipping in: not taking breaks and slouching while typing or using the mouse. By the end of day two I was super exhausted and in a modicum of pain—nothing a paracetamol or two and rest wouldn't fix. But still, I was very proud of what I had achieved.

By the end of day three I felt as though I was having a heart attack on the incorrect side of my body. Pecs, ribs, scapula, rhomboids . . . you name the muscle group or connective tissue and it was staging a mutiny. At this point we'd gotten physical therapy appointments out to every three weeks. I had my six-month check up with my surgeon the next day, and even she was pointing out which of my muscle groups needed more attention. She said that perhaps I had overdone it with my work plan.

Off I went to see my physiotherapist, and what do you know—yup, overdid it. And not only was I back to weekly appointments, but I was also taped up so I couldn't raise my arm above my head and my rhomboids and scapula had extra support. Well done, P-A! But never fear, there are unexpected benefits to causing myself so much grief. I was able to prove to myself that my pain, fatigue and physical limitations were not simply in my head, and that well-trained others saw the consequences of my testing my physical abilities. My psych calls this a turning point.

Once again, I found the positive. I was able to use this information to work with my exercise physiologist and physiotherapist to develop a specific muscle-strengthening rehab program just for me. I've always been partial to lifting weights, and this is now what I have to do to ensure I can physically function within society. I have twice-weekly rehab appointments and I have so many pieces of gym equipment in my house these days I am able to do my own at-home circuit training. Throw in a bit of chakra balancing dancing and Tai Chi and we're mind, body and soul spirited.

The rebuilding process could take absolutely years to work through, but once again I'm here to do this. I may live with the daily pain, fatigue and the need to implement MacGyver techniques to achieve standard daily tasks—anything from putting on deodorant to drying my hair to putting on clothes over my head to attempting to hang clothes on the line can all lead to rib-popping, among other things—my team have certainly been the one constant that has kept me hanging on to the surfboard through treatment and post-treatment.

Another interesting component which my physical treatment team and I have been working through is something I call 'Buddha Belly'.

I coined this phrase the day after my bilateral. I still had the compression bandage on and all I could see was a rather expansive belly where once all I could see was breasty dumplings. At that stage I knew it was more expansive than it should've been, as in bloated, not just fat, but I did not know it would have a mind of its own. I decided it needed a use, so rubbing it for good luck was it, hence Buddha Belly. Little did I know rubbing Buddha Belly was a way of controlling it too. I truly am quite intuitive some days!

Before my diagnosis, I was completely unaware of the role your mammary glands play in lymphatic drainage, and once you do not have them anymore, where does the drainage go? I quickly discovered, for me and many others, that it goes to my belly. The things you don't read about when you're newly diagnosed and grappling with that means for you and your treatment and recovery.

My surgeon told me compression knickers would become my friends. I grumbled and cursed at this, at the time thinking, *I am forty-five, too young for compression knickers.* Turns out compression is fantastic for quelling Buddha Belly, as it gets everything moving and draining. I am still working on becoming friends with compression knickers. I personally prefer to dress knowing that at any given moment Buddha Belly may appear from nowhere and accentuate other lovelier features of my person. Have I mentioned I love my shoulders?

Once again, my physical therapy team have been truly amazing in assisting me to understand what is going on and how I can help my body adjust to its new version of itself.

On the eve of my first birthday post-surgery, I was sitting in a local park watching the full moon rise over the ocean. A group of senior hipsters asked if they could use the bench and table I was perched at the end of to have their wine and cheese while they too watched the moon rise. Naturally I said yes. They then asked if I would like to join them, and one of the ladies stated they had food and drink that was okeh when you are pregnant too. I looked at her and smiled, laughed a wee bit, and said, 'I'm not pregnant.' The mortified look she had made me smile. She came flying around my side of the table, held my hand and apologised profusely, and I simply said, 'I'm not pregnant, I just don't have boobs anymore, and I get Buddha Belly as a consequence.'

All the ladies piped in and started asking lots of questions, as a friend of theirs had just had a single mastectomy and they thought she had simply put on weight—yup, don't get me started on that statement.

So with the knowledge my treatment team had provided me to date, I became a living community-service announcement. While I have no idea if their friend's treatment regimen was one of the ones which increase weight—and I made them all very aware that I couldn't comment on their friend's treatment—I was grateful that I was able to impart some new knowledge for them based on my experience.

I don't know if Buddha Belly and I will ever part company. But as with every component of the fine print, I am discovering I am simply working through what's best for me. And this is all I recommend that anyone else achieve: what is best for you and your newfound stylish authenticity. For me, I have physio-administered lymphatic drainage treatments and specific daily, self-administered lymphatic massage. I eat an alkaline diet and, when it's happening more frequently, I use naturopathic preparations. And yes, I am working towards compression knickers.

One of the funniest components of the fine print for me has been the physics. Or perhaps even a wee bit of chemistry, as this bit involves equilibrium and balance.

Again, the science is fascinating. Think logically about what would normally occur if one was to instantly remove 6 kg from the front of any object. Its balance would suddenly require recalibration, equilibrium would be skewwhiff and the centre of gravity goneski. So why didn't it occur to me that would happen to me? My ballast was listing, so to speak.

Some seven years down the track and I am still falling over. It's quite hilarious. I will be walking, and the wings will come out to stabilise me. And when I say wings, I mean my arms, not actual wings. Naturally, all the work I am doing with my posture and muscle groups and connective tissue is assisting this greatly, along with all the strength-building exercises.

Losing your balance is simply another one of the fine-print things that don't occur to you until you are actually living the consequences.

And sometimes those consequences leave additional scarring. Yes, there has been more than one occasion when my wing expansion wasn't fast enough and there has been subsequent face-planting. The most hilarious happened after I returned to work. I was walking with my manager after finishing an onsite workday. My body decided my forehead needed to find the only concrete lintel of the fences we were walking adjacent to. So that listing day ended up with permanent scars over my eye, concussion, a tetanus shot, black eyes and my manager starting the process to medically retire me. I was now a 'work hazard'—lovingly said, of course.

Your centre of gravity being different also affects the way you walk: your gait and arm movements. I get blisters from shoes that I never got blisters from previously, and in places I have never had blisters, and it's all attributed to the change in my centre of gravity.

To quote The Gait Guys (physios who specialise in exploring the links between human movement, biomechanics and gait): 'Bottom line, every external and internal parameter that changes affects the human organism and thus affects their gait.' Imagine if I was to have reconstruction or wear prosthesis, I would be changing my gait all over again and send everything out of whack all over again.

The physical side of the fine print is fascinating from a science-nerd point of view; however, it can be simply confronting from a day-to-day-living point of view. I won't lie, you do on occasion need additional energy to remain positive and hang on to the surfboard. One of my team verbalised recently how long I could be working to retrain my body physically, and let's just say I really do hope I'm around to see it back in place. Yes, it's going to take *that* long. But I am always learning, which I am grateful for.

Without my physical treatment team, I certainly wouldn't be as far as I am, nor would I have learnt as much as I have about our fascinating bodies. My wish for everyone is to find a specialist rehab and physical treatment team to work with during your treatment and recovery. In

Australia and New Zealand, look for PINC & STEEL International physios if you can.[1] Most of all, make sure everyone is working with you to ensure you are the best version of your authentic self you can be, despite everything that is going on.

---

1   www.pincandsteel.com

Keep on moving

As I mentioned a wee bit earlier, on my way to have my bilateral mastectomy, the tune playing in my mum's car was 'All About That Bass'. Poignant. But wait, it gets better. This was also the tune playing in my mum's car when she collected me from hospital post mastectomy. I can sense a soul message brewing! My mum is a wee bit groovy on occasion, but she certainly only listens to the radio. Then, wait for it, following 'All About That Bass' came 'Keep On Movin'' by Five. I firmly believe my intuition chats to me through music. Yells, most days. This was one of the yelling days. Putting aside the stay-flat message briefly, moving is certainly the key to survival long-term, and in all ways: emotional, physical and spiritual.

To start with, let's get physical.

Cast your mind back to a few months after my bilateral mastectomy, when I was en route to rejoining the world as a 'real woman' and on the reconstruction path. I was gently informed that to achieve reconstruction I had to lose a gazillion and one kilos, which would accomplish this alleged dream of being 'normal'. Enter stage left my EPE: exercise physiologist extraordinaire. My life has never been the same.

Her first challenge was to navigate P-A being told she *had* to lose weight once again. My introduction to weight loss was in vitro—my mother was placed on a 1,000-calorie diet when she was pregnant with me due to high blood pressure. Days after I was born, my mother was presented with my first diet schedule, or menu, from the nursing team. Being a baby just shy of ten pounds, I apparently required certain foods and in certain portions. And while this menu may have been a laugh for the nursing team, it set the scene for my life. The doctor who delivered me also referred to me as the 'monster' due to my size, and often suggested to my parents that I would probably end up making a great front-row forward. So my poor EPE, like my BCN who delivered the original weight loss message, had to navigate over forty-five years of associated emotional baggage.

Her second challenge: my dodgy pre- and post-bilateral limbs.

I had never encountered an Accredited Exercise Physiologist (AEP) before this. I'd had an amazing personal trainer years earlier but had no idea what an AEP did. I do now. And seriously, if you do nothing other than finding an AEP who understands the consequences of a mastectomy, your life will be so much simpler, fuller and stronger. A quick note though: I have the *only* EPE!

So a few months after my bilateral, I toddled off to meet the exercise physiologist who worked with my physiotherapist to see if she could achieve where years of alleged failure persisted. Seven years down the track I am still working with my EPE, so I can live the fullest life possible, and not just physically. She definitely achieved.

Over the years she has introduced me to many new and exciting concepts to assist in my ongoing recovery, and living in general.

Number one is 'just keep moving'. She was a researcher on the international study which discovered that exercise and movement decreases the possibility of breast cancer reoccurrence—i.e., your cancer cells going rogue on you again.

According to Cancer Australia:

> One of the most common concerns for women following treatment for breast cancer is uncertainty about the future and fear of a recurrence. The evidence suggests that there are some lifestyle factors such as physical activity that may reduce the risk of breast cancer coming back after women have finished their treatment.

Studies of physical activity in women after breast cancer have shown some striking findings. In a recent meta-analysis of observational studies which looked at over 10,000 women after breast cancer diagnosis, even moderate physical activity was shown to reduce risk of recurrence of breast cancer by 24% and reduce risk of death from breast cancer by 34%.

A more recent study of around 3,000 women also confirms that activity such as just 3 hours a week of brisk exercise can reduce risk of breast cancer mortality by 30%.

This could mean that women who feel well enough could undertake some regular exercise such as going for a 30-minute brisk walk several times a week, going for a bike ride or doing some strength training. It could also mean undertaking some activities such as dancing or taking the dog for a walk may also help you stay healthy.[2]

This seemingly innocuous piece of information changed my world and the focus of my treatment. It did take a few months to realise the importance of this information. I didn't have to be doing exercise to achieve a weight-loss goal for someone else. I didn't have to be undergoing the struggle with my brain every time I exercised, that inner monologue asking me why I always had to lose weight for other people.

It was simple: I didn't. If I want to be around as long as possible, to annoy as many people as possible, then exercise and movement are the keys. And yes, I've always known movement played its role, like everyone else who grow up in Norm's 'Life. Be In It' era. However, this information about movement was revolutionary for me. My mindset was now in a type of survival mode. It was in the 'no, cancer cells, you will not go rogue

---

2   Recurrent and metastatic cancer: Cancer Australia: accessed 12 December 2021

again. Thank you kindly. Cheers, taaaaa' mode now. And while hanging out in survival mode is also not healthy in the long term, I was grateful for the ability to hang out here, as it gave me clarity. Exercise became my friend. It was no longer a consequence of my lifelong weight-loss Achilles heel being poked. It was a huge component of cancer prevention, and the science backed it up.

Knowing that exercise and movement are keys to preventing cancer reoccurrence and overall prevention made challenge number one redundant for my newly acquired EPE. She's very clever. In one statement, she was able to wipe away forty-five-plus years of emotional blocks. Don't get me wrong, these certainly do rear their collective heads every now and again. But knowing how I can do something for myself to assist in preventing my cancer cells going rogue again is a great way to deal with their head-rearing, swiftly and precisely.

And this is not just a long-term prevention strategy. Exercise after your initial treatment is fantastic for so many areas of your life and cancer-related side effects. The BCNA website is a wonderous place for insightful information, and they share the following about exercise:

> Getting regular exercise during and following your breast cancer treatment can have many benefits. It can improve your physical and emotional wellbeing and improve quality of life. Exercise can help manage treatment and cancer related side effects such as fatigue, pain and lymphoedema and lowered bone density. It can also improve mood, sleep, body weight, muscle strength, confidence, depression and anxiety. There is very strong evidence that targeted exercise can also reduce the risk of breast cancer recurrence.[3]

---

3   Exercise and staying fit: Breast Cancer Network Australia (bcna.org.au) accessed 12 December 2021

Armed with this newfound knowledge, I dove right in, walking every day, strength-training every second day and Pilates and weights with my EPE once a week. As a consequence of my drive to survive, the weight came off too.

Over the past seven years, I have lost and gained weight a few times. However, the difference is I now know why. As soon as I stop moving in the best ways for me, the weight creeps back. And I'm actually okeh with this. As generally it coincides with another round of surgery, surgery-induced menopause, tearing my meniscus, fracturing a knee bone or even a trauma-inducing event. And yes, all of these are real-life P-A scenarios. I have also undertaken three charity walks in this time, two with my EPE, something I would never have considered pre-mastectomy. And I am currently training my knees to achieve the next charity walk.

The bottom line is that I know I have to keep moving to keep rogue cells at bay and to build upper-body strength to achieve the everyday activities we all take for granted.

Challenge number two was the dodgy limbs pre- and post-mastectomy. I've had dodgy knees since, hmm ... birth, probably, thanks to genetics and falling over a lot as a young kid. I had an arthroscopy to clean up one of my knees when I was sixteen, and as a consequence I was never meant to kneel or squat ever again, or do breaststroke in the pool—a rather specific direction at the time. And then there was a violent car crash in my thirties, which really stuffed up one of my knees. So basically, due to some genetics and a lot of external trauma, I have minimal cartilage left in my knees and tri-compartmental osteoarthritis in both of them. Oh, and I have genetically super flat feet too, which is not helpful for knees and hips.

Post-mastectomy, it's rare for us to not have upper-body strength issues. Keep your eyes open for this, *please*. Mine are predominantly with rib movement, pecs, rhomboids, lats and rotator cuffs. You lose upper-body movement and strength as a consequence of a mastectomy and the associated scar tissue. But I do have core muscles, which I use often.

And how did my EPE get around the whole dodgy P-A limb issues? Quite simply, really. This is actually the point of seeing an Accredited Exercise Physiologist: they know your muscles. They see your muscles. They can see movement you didn't realise could occur. (Unless you are wearing striped clothing, which has been banned from our EPE classes.)

Intriguingly, there is a great deal of cognitive work involved in a session with an AEP, activating and pushing individual muscles in singular movements. So there I was, with my newfound attitude towards exercise and movement, and hungry to learn what I could actually achieve with my dodgy limbs. Lots of things, it turns out. I fell in love with the reformer and stability chair, and even have one in my house these days. My passion for lifting heavy objects on the ends of bars and pulling them down from overhead was re-ignited. I've been introduced to the world of crazy moves such as superman, swan, pike and dead bugs. And I love every moment of it. Predominantly, the focus is on strength-building, whether that be for my chest/thoracic areas or my knees, but what I marvel at every session is my EPE's ability to work with where my body is at on that particular day. Yes, she has learnt the P-A tell expressions which indicate my mind is saying yes and my body is saying *'Ohhhhh, heeeell noooooo!'* But she is equipped to work through everything we throw at her.

Since having my original bilateral mastectomy, I have had a revision to remove more stuff, and the excess skin left for reconstruction. The associated scar tissue has led to permanent issues with my strength and movement on my right-hand side. I've also had two rounds of gynaecological surgery due to suspected endometrial cancer, which led to loss of strength in my core and pelvic area and, like most breast cancer survivors, early onset menopause (surgically induced for me), which can lead to bone density issues, heart issues and insulin intolerance. Exercise and movement are keys to keeping strong and healthy after all this surgery. They also assist with maintaining a positive outlook and mental well-being.

While the additional surgeries have thrown curveballs our way, like inevitable weight gain due to not being able to exercise while my body recovers from the trauma of surgery, working with my EPE and being a sponge for all the knowledge she wishes to share has made me excited to share that at no point has my brain reverted back to the previous weight-loss mentality. Well, not permanently. There was a moment prior to my hysterectomy and oophorectomy when I was told to lose weight again to ensure a good recovery. After the inevitable pouting and feet stamping about once again being told to lose weight for a somewhat mythical reason (as the request is always based on the BMI issue), with the assistance of my EPE I was able to regroup my thinking to being healthy and strong for surgery. The scales may not have moved down too much, but my body composition certainly changed and I was strong enough to not have to rely on my core muscles for the twelve weeks post-surgery, despite extra dodgy knees and popping ribs.

To be blunt, my EPE keeps me sane most weeks. About four years after my initial surgery, I was medically retired and subsequently the recipient of a disability pension. I am eternally grateful for the financial assistance, although the reasons for the retirement are challenging every day, especially when you are a writer by trade and passion. Without going into too much detail, the rib-popping and movement limitations are all pain-inducing and sometimes unbearable, breath-taking pain. The pain is there all day, every day, and then sometimes just for good measure it kicks in at an extra-high level just to remind your brain that your body doesn't appreciate doing certain movements anymore.

Initially, one of the main things I was hoping I may be able to regain by working with my EPE and physio was working at a computer the same way I did pre-mastectomy (read: thirteen hours a day). Crazy times. And while thirteen hours is a ridiculous amount, it is what my job and life entailed back then. As I mentioned, prior to returning to work I did the gradual testing of what my body could withstand. My EPE was also able to provide me with the proper posture- and pain-management exercises to ensure that I could achieve some of my previous duties.

Sadly, my body decided that returning to my former work persona was not going to be achievable, let alone sustainable. For almost two years I attempted to achieve the same work output in fewer working hours. I could do about twenty minutes continuously and then take a twenty-minute break. This makes a 7.15-hour stint a reeaaally long day, which then has flow-on effects, mentally and emotionally. Within a couple of months of returning to work, I had to take another extended break to try to recover. I returned in a part-time capacity and then worked permanently from home. And my hours kept being dropped to the point where it became clear to my boss and my treatment team that, as much as I tried, my return to work was an epic fail.

All through this, my EPE had my back, as did my physiotherapist. My home office has numerous pieces of equipment such as stretchy bands pulleys, small malleable balls, even smaller spikey balls, light weights, a bench seat that morphs into a weight bench or as a streamlined reformer for core work, a BOSU and a giant ball along with specifically designed P-A program to undertake stretches and strength-building to realign my ribs as much as I can during my breaks between work sessions.

Yes, this is me and my EPE, Kelly Prosser from Fluid Health Co., showing off my amazing lat-pulldown ability. Scan the code for more info on FHCo and exercise physiology.

And this setup exists to this day. I have no vision of it ever changing. I may no longer be able to work consistently, and I never know on any given day what my work capacity may be; however, when I do undertake writing it is under strict practices to limit the effect on my body, mind and spirit. And ever so oddly, for a writer in particular, I have come to really enjoy the interval way of undertaking computer work and the twenty-minute sprint sessions of writing followed by a twenty-minute cooldown. In fact, as a writer I use these times to clarify what I have written and what I am going to write next. This is the unexpected magic my EPE has brought to my daily regimen, and I am forever grateful.

Right, and now I'm off to do some band stretching and ball-hugging. What can I say, I'm a creature of good habits now. And the other thing I will say: add an AEP to your treatment team and your toolkit *now!*

Colour my world

I recently made a bold statement: I love colour! The person I said this to responded, 'And yet you wear a lot of black.' They were completely correct, of course, I do wear a lot of black. And that's because I *can*. Not everyone can, you see. And it also doesn't mean I do not love colour. Psychologically, black clothing represents keeping people at arm's length as well—a classic introvert's trick!

However, while I may outwardly wear black 99 percent of the time, if one looks very closely they will see the colour I need in my world on that particular day on my person too. There's always purple somewhere, generally in the shape of amethyst jewellery, and don't forget undergarments, folks—they could possibly be incredibly bright and colourful and you simply wouldn't know.

So why would I make such a bold statement about loving colour? Well, here's the thing colour is simply amazing. And I should divulge right about now that I am actually a colour therapist and analyst before I start banging on about how fab colour is. And a caveat: this is where I may go all sciencey on you again.

Understanding colour and how to use it is yet another tool that helps me muddle through treatment and life. I would be lost without my colour knowledge; it's a lifelong obsession as well. It is one of the easiest ways to feel fabulous every day, even assisting you to bring yourself out of the treatment-regimen mud and thrive.

Let's get the science stuff out of the way—an abridged physics lesson, if you will. So, within the universe, positive and negative charges (waves of energy) are constantly vibrating and producing electromagnetic waves travelling at an incredibly high speed. Each of these waves has a different wavelength and speed of vibration. Together they form part of the electromagnetic spectrum, and this is where colour lives. The spectrum has visible and invisible components. The visible component is what we perceive as colour, or visible light energy.

Visible light energy is made up of many frequencies and wavelengths, falls between infrared and ultraviolet and each colour has a different wavelength and frequency. Higher-frequency colours—violet, indigo, blue—have smaller wavelengths and higher levels of energy and are more harmful—think UV rays. Lower frequency colours—yellow, orange, red—have longer wavelengths and lower levels of energy and are harmless. Green is smack in the middle, and balanced between higher and lower.

From a psychology point of view, many studies have been undertaken to determine the effect colour has on folks from an emotional and psychological point of view. One of the most prominent in these circles is Jules B. Davidoff, professor of psychology and director of the Centre for Cognition, Computation and Culture, Goldsmiths University of London. They do fascinating research, which I would urge anyone to look into. For example, there is a causal effect for saying things like 'feeling blue' or why medical facilities shouldn't be decorated in certain shades of green.

Are you now gaining a sense of why I love colour? It permeates all areas of our lives. Colour is a powerful, natural form of universal energy. It surrounds us every day and is essential to our well-being.

Colour may shape what we are attracted too and what repels us. I personally have a complete aversion to pink. I know, it's bit ironic really given the overall topic of this book. In particular, pink food. Not salmon pink—I love salmon—but that beetroot-juice-has-leaked-and-made-everything-pink pink. And yes, even pink cake icing is icky to me. It's simply not a natural colour people. And before anyone who knows colour as much as me goes 'arrrhhhhh hold on . . .', technically both salmon and beetroot aren't pink either. Salmon is a version of orange and beetroot falls into the red/purple category. I am simply using these two food groups as easily recognisable examples of how pink repels me.

Now if I truly had my counsellor/colour therapist hat on right now, I could go into the whys and wherefores about my pink aversion; however, I shall spare you that detail. Suffice to say we all truly have colours that we are drawn to and ones we are not, and for definitive reasons these factors affect who we are and how we respond to events in our world.

And although there are numerous factors which will influence our environments daily, colour is clearly quite a significant one. Colours evoke different reactions and can range from relaxing, energizing or stimulating surroundings to aggravating, draining and boring ones.

I firmly believe in using the energies of light and colour to harmonise the body, mind and soul. For example, the use of red grabs our attention and may stimulate or aggravate our being, whereas the use of blue may calm or relax us, and yellow makes most of us think of warm, joyful, sunshiny days.

Sticking with the pink theme, take for example a colour called Baker-Miller pink. In common terms it is a bubble-gum colour, and its name comes from the scientists who researched its psychological properties and uses. It is also referred to as 'Drunk Tank Pink', as the scientists discovered that, when the drunk tanks—i.e., holding cells—on a naval base were painted this colour, the occupants' aggressive behaviour dissipated. After further research, it was discovered this colour has the same effect on people generally, and has subsequently been used in numerous crime-prevention campaigns and even prison uniforms, although most folks think erroneously that this is to belittle the prisoners. You simply cannot become angry around this colour in all its pinkness, even me.

By embracing the full range of colour in their appropriate proportions and harmonies, we can achieve balance and harmony in many areas of life, such as passion, zest, warmth, relaxation, nourishment, nurturing, introspection and spirituality.

The bottom line for me is that colour is light, and if we were to be deprived of light—colour—we would experience significant physiological and psychological disturbances. Think seasonal affective disorder, folks.

Colour permeates our lives in many different ways, such as the colour of a room, or the colours we are innately drawn to or repelled by in clothing, food and art. For example, yellow is great for a study as it stimulates your brain to learn, but not so great in a bedroom for the exact same reason or if you happen to be ADHD. Another example is if you happen to be overheating or have a temperature, stay away from red foods, as they are warming. Use blue foods to calm down and green foods to balance. Examples of blue foods include blueberries, some plums and eggplants. And just so you know, blue foods are more a blue/indigo colour. All of the ways we receive colour in our lives have an influence on our cognition and well-being.

When you are undergoing your treatment schedule, having knowledge of how colour can assist you—whether it be the colour of the room you are recovering in, or food you are eating to assist with side effects of treatment, or the clothes you are wearing—can be very helpful. The power of colour is phenomenal.

And now for my favourite use of colour, and the most useful tool I have in my thriving post-mastectomy kit: knowing how to use colour in clothing to bring out the best in me.

For those of us old enough to remember the 1980s, a wee bit of a colour revolution occurred. More so in the United States and Europe, but nonetheless, many of us had our colours done. I was sixteen at the time, and my entire family had theirs done. It was an absolute revelation to me. I suddenly discovered that colour can be the most flattering tool in your wardrobe, and is the best tool to complement your natural beauty. Not only did knowing my colours open up my world of style, it has saved me money over the years, as I haven't spent hard-earned cash on clothing just because it is in fashion that season. Basically, if it's not my colour I don't buy it.

Colours simplify your life, your wardrobe, your makeup and your hair-colour choices, for those of us who are at an age when one chooses to enhance one's natural colour—if one can actually remember it, of course!

I'm sounding like an old school pyramid marketing sales rep, aren't I? Bear with me. As you may have picked up by now, I have chosen to not have reconstruction after my bilateral mastectomy. And I also make the choice daily not to wear prostheses, purely because I feel so conspicuous wearing them.

So how does colour help with this, you ask? Brilliant question indeed. It really is simple: if you know your best colours—and I will go into a wee bit of detail soon, really I will—then this is what reflects on your face and suddenly, magically, it becomes the centre of attention and you quite literally glow.

Wearing the best colour for you means the focus is on your beautiful face and not your clothing or physique. And while not hiding the fact that I no longer have breasts and it's my choice to go out into the world with my concave chest, I certainly do not purposely draw attention to these physical attributes. I have very Victorian sensibilities; I had the same approach to dressing pre-mastectomy. One of the best ways to achieve this is through wearing the best colours for you.

As I mentioned earlier in this chapter, I am a colour therapist and analyst. I was a colour therapist—that's the sciencey stuff—prior to my diagnosis, and I can guarantee this has been helpful in regaining balance and harmony in my physical, emotional and mental well-being. And although I have been a 'wearing the best colour' convert for nearly four decades now (geezzz I'm old), it wasn't until after my surgery I rediscovered the benefits of knowing what colours work, and off I toddled to become a colour analyst, predominantly so I could share this knowledge with the world and assist others in enhancing their natural beauty, irrespective of what circumstances they find themselves in.

I studied the 4-Seasons version, as it is the easiest to understand. It's the original and, well, for me it's possibly my favourite tool in my Elegantly Unique Toolkit to assist in regaining confidence outwardly after a bilateral mastectomy. Mind you, it's definitely not limited to our arena—colour may be used to assist in regaining confidence in your stylish and authentic self, no matter what the circumstances.

And because I love sharing knowledge . . . what is the 4-seasons method? While not wishing to sound offhanded and glib, it truly is simple—if you are trained correctly, of course. A colour analyst, like *moi*, throws some drapes under your chin to reflect light back onto your face, or is able simply to look at you and ask certain questions, and we work out with you what colours are best for you and which ones may not be. Mind you, I personally believe you wear what you want; however, I can show you why the best colours are the best for you.

The 4-seasons are obviously winter, summer, autumn and spring. Winter and summer are the cool-based colours, and autumn and spring are the warm-based ones. And before folks start having kittens about summer being a cool-based colour range, these are based on European seasons, not Australian. So we are talking about the brilliant intensities of black and white for winter, the soft pastel shades of summer, the rich earthy tones of autumn, and the vibrant, clear, warm colours of spring.

When it comes to colours, we all know our likes and dislikes; however, knowing your actual colours opens up all the in-betweens. Like for me, the pink despiser, I own magenta-coloured clothing, which may be commonly described as hot pink and I look fabulous in it, as I am a winter and it's part of my colour palette. Thankfully, black and royal purple are too, or I would have been a devastated sixteen-year-old, I can tell you!

When you are wearing the best colour for you, be ready to receive compliments on how healthy you look, or that you are shining. The things you and everyone else will notice are:

- ♥ Your eyes sparkle
- ♥ Your skin appears clearer
- ♥ Your hair is brighter—yes, I know, this is subject to what your treatment plan is
- ♥ Your complexion is smooth and clarified
- ♥ Lines, shadows and circles on your face are minimised
- ♥ Your face has a healthy glow
- ♥ Your beautiful glowing face becomes the focus of attention

Now, if you are not wearing the best colour, you may get the 'you look tired' comments, or the 'are you okily dokily?' question or a positive statement which really isn't, although you may not know this, as you'll likely hear the dreaded 'that's a great dress, shirt, top, etc.' What this means is your face has disappeared, and all that is noticeable if the item of clothing instead of you in all your gorgeousness.

Why does your face disappear when you are wearing a colour that is not optimal for you? The things you and everyone else will notice are:

- ♥ The colour of your outfit becomes the focal point and pushes your beautiful face into the background
- ♥ Accentuation of shadows, lines, blemishes and discolouration on your face
- ♥ See more lines and shadows around your mouth and nose, even if they are not normally visible to the naked eye
- ♥ Dark circles under your eyes are accentuated
- ♥ Your face may age, and you may look too weak or too strong
- ♥ And to be honest, you may simply feel frumpy for no apparent reason.

Learning to use colour confidently, we are able to express our individuality and build a strong and positive self-image. In other words, we regain our confidence through being stylish and authentic. Colours in harmony with your colour palette will enhance your natural beauty and individuality. Your unique style and authenticity are emphasised, not what you are wearing—or in many of our cases, what we are *not* wearing. Did I mention I have chosen to stay flat and not wear prostheses?

So, I know my colours—when are you getting yours done, hey?

Pear-shaped? Seriously?

The one statement throughout all of my treatment that sent me reeling was: 'You're now pear-shaped.' I didn't have my shoulders amputated, just my boobs.

It was this simple statement that changed my life path, and I am truly grateful for this, once I got over the magnitude of the statement, that is.

I've never been one to understand why people feel it is their right to tell others what body shape or size they perceive another person to be. As someone who always been outside of the 'norm' when it comes to body shape and size, perhaps I have more baggage around this issue than your average person, but even so, telling someone this is simply a judgement and an unsolicited opinion.

Even the ongoing debate about what determines 'plus size' is completely confounding to me. I'm just shy of six-foot, in old money, and I have lived up to that description the doctor who delivered me gave my parents: 'She's going to make a good front-row forward'. So apparently I have been 'plus size' my entire life. What I have never fathomed is why folks feel they have the right to categorise and make such judgements. I understand the concept of providing clothing sizes; however, I seriously wish there was some conformity. Can they not simply be *sizes* instead of petite, normal and plus labelling, which adds to someone's self-worth and self-esteem issues?

Where is this rant going, exactly? Great question. It's simple, really: style equals confidence, not fashion. I have always believed this and have never been a follower of fashion. I have discovered since having a bilateral mastectomy that this rings even truer—style is definitely confidence.

After my mastectomy, I was suddenly confronted with having a wardrobe full to the brim of clothing for a busty hourglass—think pinup-girl style meets London Mod—while needing a wardrobe for a curvy hourglass who no longer had the breasty dumplings to fill out the busty bits. Many have described my style over the years as elegant and graceful. And suddenly I found myself in a world of clothing suggestions and style suggestions that were so divorced from my actual style that I could literally feel my confidence and elegance slipping away drip by drip.

Being the previous owner of very large breasts, I have never worn light-coloured tops or frills or cowl necklines, let alone button-up shirts. And it was these shirts that started my style loss. I will admit there is a practicality to them, as when one has a mastectomy one has drains and stitches and scars which all equal arms not being able to reach above one's head, so buttoned-up tops it was. But seriously, this was only while I had the drains in. I have learnt yet more MacGyver manoeuvres to ensure I didn't have to continue wearing the buttons, despite still having limited arm range.

In the early years post-mastectomy, I was certainly becoming more and more withdrawn due to my perception that I should be conforming to a style to hide my lack of breasts. And strangely enough, it was when I was being fitted for my prostheses (the ones I owned, chose not to wear and subsequently gave to a local charity) that I rediscovered my shoulders. I love my shoulders and always have. Shoulders feature prominently in the style I have developed over many years. Again, think pinup, think Bardot—as in Brigitte, not that interesting singing group.

This is when I realised I could re-invent my style, based on my tastes as opposed to succumbing to the judgements and the hiding-your-lack-of-breasts suggestions of others, let alone the perilous idea of 'what's in fashion'. And the huge positive in this was that, to accentuate my beloved shoulders, I didn't have to hide or conceal bra straps anymore!

It was about this time I remembered that I am a dressmaker. I know how to make clothes. I have been making my own clothes since I was seven, in fact, as I could never find anything that quite fit me off the shelf. I was too tall, too busty, too curvy, too Marilyn in proportions. I suddenly realised I could confidently regain my style.

And this is when that comment appeared. I was discussing my excitement at working out how to regain my style while staying flat and, *bang*, 'P-A you have to accept you're now a pear shape,' was dropped in the chat. *Arrrrhhhh*. Hell no, I do not. From my trillion years of measuring and sewing I know that to determine that body shape it is the proportion of hips to waist to shoulders. And I hadn't had my shoulders removed, so how was I suddenly a pear shape? I have subsequently undertaken a style course to re-affirm that I am not being belligerent in my thought process. Strangely, I am not. And I can gleefully confirm I am an X-shape, or 'hourglass', in olden-days' terminology—albeit a slightly less exaggerated version of an hourglass.

What does one do with this information, however? It's not simply to prove you're right and the comment-dropper is wrong. Well, there may have been a wee bit of that—I know, that's wrong. What one really does is start the wardrobe cull, and one focuses on working out what one's style is, or how to regain it to fit the new version of your body.

The wardrobe cull is confronting. Please know this and prepare yourself for it. A big box of tissues is required, as even I cried. Yes, me.

Those who know me well will be going, *Really?* right about now. Basically the wardrobe cull is the physical admission that you are not the person you were. Grief kicks in about now. And while this is a positive from a release-and-moving-forward point of view, it is quite confronting.

In fact, I undertook the wardrobe cull over a twelve-month period, as I simply couldn't bear to part with some of my pinup dresses, especially the ones I purchased from the USA. Many an hour was spent trying to work out how I could modify them to fit, or if I should wear a belt, or if I should wear my prostheses—an option I briefly entertained. So many what-ifs involved. All up, I have basically given away my entire wardrobe, almost twenty green shopping bags filled with clothes—oh, and the gorgeous bras. My nieces, cousins, aunty, mum, cousin's friends, folks in Bali and numerous charities have all received a part of my former life, and this fills me with joy. Out of a seemingly unhappy circumstance I was able to bring smiles to other people's faces by sharing the elegance.

And now that my wardrobe is bereft of my former life, what do I replace it with? This has definitely been the extra-fun bit! Although, it's been once again confronting and eye-opening at the same time. I have had suggestions from 'Wear frills to hide your lack of cleavage' to 'You can wear scarves to hide your lack of cleavage' right through to 'Well, you'll just have to wear your prostheses to make that one fit properly'. No. Just no. This is about *my* style. *My* grace. *My* elegance. Not anyone else's. The cookie-cutter approach was once again rearing its ugly head.

I feel it takes great strength to stand up against what others perceive you should be doing and the judgement of others to ensure you are being your authentic and stylish self. And this is exactly the approach I take.

I liked my style prior to having the girls amputated, I really did. So why do I need to change my clothing style simply because the clothing you can buy off the shelf doesn't automatically accommodate broad shoulders and a concave chest (not simply a small bust)? It took me changing my mindset and remembering what I had learnt over a trillion years of dressmaking to be able to feel stylish, authentic, elegant and graceful once again.

This is what I did, with a little of bit of nudging from the style tips of one of my gurus, Gok Wan:

- ♥ I actually try clothes on now. I despise this, but I force myself to do it as I don't know what works now. I have a general idea based on my body shape, and I know how to emphasise and diminish using various cuts, styles, fabrics, etc., but unless I own a similar garment, I try it on.

- ♥ After trying on clothes, if I find something doesn't fit me the way it used too, I analyse the shape of the clothing, not *my* shape. For example, I have broad shoulders, and my hips match them. I cannot automatically decrease the clothing size for my top simply because I no longer have breasts—I still have shoulders. The consequence of the extra material around the chest is that the waist ends up nearer your hips. You are then suddenly confronted with an entire inner monologue about how much weight you have gained for the top to be so tight around your abdomen and hip area. Let me tell you this: *you haven't gained weight*. It took this dressmaker a while to work out was going on, but as soon as I did I added these styles to the 'Hmm . . . I'll ponder before buying' list. It's the same with garments which have breast darts, high waists, bust-line gathers and princess-seam styles.

- ♥ I emphasise my shoulders. Did I mention I love my shoulders? And I have re-discovered that showing your shoulders and a wee bit of your décolletage is quite alluring, almost—dare I say it—sexy.

- ♥ I make sure I am wearing the best colour to harmonise with my skin. This instantly puts the focus on my glowing face as opposed to the clothes I am wearing highlighting all the parts of my body which are missing.

- ♥ I ensure my clothes actually fit me. I am well known for buying and wearing clothing a number of sizes too big for me. When clothes fit well, you avoid feeling the frumpies.
- ♥ I do wear scarves. In winter. To keep me warm.
- ♥ I wear pinup and London '60s mod styles because I can and I feel good in them. I always have, and why change my entire style due to something that happened to me? Work your style to work with what you have now!
- ♥ I also have styles which accommodate the Buddha Belly moments, so I can avoid the 'are you pregnant?' questions as much as possible.
- ♥ I dress my personality. This is how I let the world know who I am without saying a word.
- ♥ I actually trust my sense of personal style. This is huge one for those of us working out where we are now based on the surgeries we have undergone. I am excited by my uniqueness, and I certainly do not want to hide it.
- ♥ I honour every part of me. If I don't, one day I'll quite possibly look back and wonder why the hell I wasted so much time worrying. Life's for living! NOW!
- ♥ Every person I have ever met wants to change at least one thing about their body. Life's too short to care about the 'are you too—?' questions.

Above all, I discovered the best accessory ever: confidence. Like me, wear yours elegantly with stylish authenticity, and I can guarantee no one will notice what is allegedly missing from your body.

I choose to simply be me. Elegantly. Stylishly.
Authentically. No boobs required.

The authentic bit: Oh, I get it now!

Have you ever quizzically and yet knowingly gone, 'Hmmm . . . really?' at a random comment made by a person you have never met? When you simply sense what is going on in your world without really understanding how you know? For me, it's understanding and following my inner voice, whether it is portraying adult, parent or child. Your intuition is the key to being authentic.

It was intuition that led me down the diagnostic path. It was intuition that made my decision to accept the clinician's bilateral advice instantly. It was ego—fear—that led me down the garden path of my initial weight loss and reconstruction choices, and it was my intuition that led me back to my 'staying flat' decision and authenticity. It was intuition that led me to the event where I met my colour analysis and style teacher and mentor, and it was intuition that led me to regain my style and just be me.

But oh boy, did I misread, ignore, completely dish my intuition most days! And working out that we are intuitive beings is a wee bit life-changing in itself. Luckily, I was already on the intuition path when I was diagnosed. But it's one I have to remember to accept and acknowledge every day.

My 'd'oh!' moment was pretty spectacular from an egoic, inauthentic point of view. A number of years ago, my younger brother was sitting in a café enjoying his double-shot soy flat white—it's oat milk these days—when a lady at the table next to him leant across and said, 'Excuse me, would you mind if I pass some information on to you?'

Not being fearful of the unknown, his answer was a resounding, 'Sure, go ahead.' He had never met this woman and he intuitively recognised she was a Reiki Master, which she confirmed.

After a short chat, with many *wow!* moments, she made the following statement to him: 'Your sister is very intuitive. Why doesn't she follow her intuition, and why isn't she sharing her light with people?'

At the same time, I was in a crystal shop purchasing amethyst earrings as a gift, and the shop assistant stared at me and all but said, 'The force is strong in you.' Out of fear—ego—I physically stepped backwards, away from the shop assistant. I simply wanted to purchase the earrings; however, it would appear the universe had decided I needed to hear other information.

After purchasing the earrings, I received a call from my brother. It started something like this, 'So, random people in coffee shops are now telling me that you need to get your act together', to which I replied, 'And random shop assistants are giving me the same message.' *Hmmm . . . really?*

So what did I do? At that point in my life I had already undertaken my level 1 Reiki attunement. However, I had become lax in my energy work and was fearful of trusting my intuition, as I was determined to focus on my fact-based career as opposed to my life purpose.

The two events which occurred to us siblings all but simultaneously led me to change my response from 'Hmmm . . . really?' to 'Oh, I get it now!' and this led me on a course of learning and discovery.

Being someone who requires tangibility in my learning, I undertook a number of diplomas to discover the fact, history and science behind my *Hmmm . . . really?* moments.

I discovered folks like Dr Carl Jung, Robert A. Johnson, Paulo Coelho and a thirteenth century Sufi poet called Hafiz. I studied Tarot, astrology, numerology, scrying, palmistry, as well as the history and science behind Hermeticism, Plato, Fibonacci and Steiner, just to name a few.

I am a qualified Reiki master and teacher, holistic counsellor, colour therapist, professional psychic and a certified angel Tarot reader—all energy-based, intuition-centric modalities. But you know what? It is the basics of simply following your gut and being your authentic self that resonates most with me and has assisted me every day through the odyssey that is breast cancer. And it is also what I feel is the most useful to everyone in the quest to believe in and trust our inner voices more fully.

Another 'a-ha' moment was inextricably linked to my discovery of celebrating my unique, authentic and stylish self. I found myself at a local psychic fair, the first one I'd been to post-diagnosis. I wasn't there for any particular reason, but as I walked in I received a metaphorical slap around the ears and subsequently booked a reading. For anyone who has ever done this, you truly don't mull over your choice of reader, as your intuition guides you to the correct one for you on that day. As I made the booking with Suzanne, whom I'd never met, the lady said to me that she reads colour cards. *Perfect,* I thought, as I love colour and its psychology.

My reading time arrived. I truly use readings as clarification sessions of information I may already know, or for information I may not have a clear view of. This reading was very different. Suzanne asked me what new business venture I was planning. As a trained reader myself, I understand these sessions are similar in format to counselling, so they require conversation. I shared with her that I was pondering assisting other young bilateral mastectomy ladies discover their new version of stylish and authentic post-treatment. I told her I was considering colour-analyst and style courses. And that's when the universe kicked in. Suzanne was a colour and style trainer, having established institutes and worked in the industry for many years. She offered to mentor me to achieve my goal. And this she did. Thanks to Suzanne and the universe, I am now a colour analyst and have a greater understanding of style.

We all follow our intuition to some degree, whether consciously or subconsciously. We are all born with intuition, and it is a misnomer to refer to some people as 'gifted' simply because they are more in tune than others. Some people are simply more naturally developed and dedicated to listen to their intuition, similar to how an Olympian is more developed physically, focused and dedicated to a goal.

The potential to be unique and special is within all of us. The courage to trust our intuition is at the centre of developing our authenticity and uniqueness.

It is up to us to focus on and listen to what is always in the background. Again, the derivation of the word itself provides the clue as to how to describe intuition. It is a Latin derivative meaning 'to look inside' or 'to contemplate'.

Numerous scholars, including Swiss psychologist Carl Jung, describe intuition as a strong form of inner wisdom, a gut feeling or a hunch, a physical sensation or even a dream. It is an ability we are all born with; however, over time many of us forget how to access and use our intuition.

Sometimes we allow our doubts and fear—ego—to take hold and question whether what we are feeling is our intuition or our imagination. Potentially, the best way to determine the difference is to be aware of the how you are feeling—do you feel at peace, confident, balanced and positive? Trust these feelings, as this is your intuition.

Second guessing your first thought, instinct or impression comes from fear and pre-conditioned judgements. Your first thought is your intuition. Be aware of it, have confidence in it and, above all, trust it.

Throughout my breast cancer odyssey, I have lost count of how many times I haven't accepted my intuition. Any time I have mentioned an ironic situation, it is basically me acknowledging that I was simply not taking notice of my intuition.

Now, with some things it took a few goes, but I did get there. And then other things—like accepting the clinician's bilateral advice, not accepting the 'you're a pear shape now' statement, attending the event where I met Suzanne, finding my treatment team, following a treatment regimen that was the correct balance of medical and complementary therapy for me to accept that I didn't have to wear prostheses to fit in—were simple and almost instantaneous acceptances of my intuition. I value the authentic Peta-Ann most.

Most of all I simply trust my intuition, and I'm continually working on lessening the fear of second-guessing myself to allow my authenticity to shine.

Never say never

Prior to my diagnosis, and while I was undergoing all the testing, I suddenly became single—a blessing in disguise, really. However, it does provide a very different set of circumstances post-surgery, whether it be support physically and emotionally right through to when you are finally getting your head around the possibility of becoming romantically involved with someone—especially someone new. The whole 'when do you tell them about your odyssey or about the scars that go from underarm to underarm or Buddha Belly or your underlying focus on preventing metastasisation in every decision you make', consciously or subconsciously.

So there I was. Post-mastectomy. Single. Almost forty-seven years old. Massive scars where the girls once inhabited. And the following statement comes floating out of my mouth during a deep and meaningful chat with one of my BFFs: 'That's it! Never again for me.' My single, crazy cat-lady life is it for me now. Unpacking this statement was a very interesting process, and a conversation I am sure many single, mastectomy owners have had with themselves, their BFFs, their family, their psych—the list goes on.

For me, finding out what is at the crux of this statement was key. When I was diagnosed, intimacy post-mastectomy wasn't a general topic of discussion, unless I chose to have the conversation with my psychiatrist. I simply added it to the 'perhaps more information should be available to women undergoing mastectomies' list. Mind you, seven years down the track, I am very excited to see the steps forward in sharing more information around the effect on relationships and sensuality through the likes of BCNA and other breast cancer research organisations.

But for ladies who feel they need to navigate the dark cloud of a potential life alone simply because an event happened to you, firstly, I would strongly suggest re-thinking this option.

Although this is not a topic I speak about with my pysch (I am positive she would be super excited if I did!), it is one I chat about with a few of my nearest and dearest. I'm not so much looking for answers from them as I am a firm believer that you have the answers inside you. It is more a way for me to collect my thoughts and work out what is actually going on for me.

Normally, I would just sit with a thought or feeling before making a decision, weighing up all options by using whatever tools I have picked up over the years to unpack what I am thinking and occasionally feeling about the situation, and any solutions or resolutions I might be able to find for myself. This is what I would regularly do: I use meditation, automatic writing, cards and pendulums and other tools from my Elegantly Unique Toolkit as my source of inspiration and direction. And yet on this occasion I had not considered any of my normal practice before boldly blurting out mid-chat: 'That's it! Never again for me.'

So where had this determination come from? Was it simply a result of years of socialisation and subsequent self-esteem issues rearing up and saying, 'Oh, please pick me'? Those pearlers of thoughts like:

- ♥ How could anyone be interested in me now?
- ♥ If I wear prostheses, when do I tell someone they're not real and in fact I have removable breasts?
- ♥ Do I get reconstruction simply as an avoidance technique to conform to an acceptable version of women in our society?

By this point in the odyssey, I had already determined I wasn't choosing to conform to society's version of normal, so it was quite confronting that this thought pattern was even making an appearance.

To be completely honest, these thoughts were not dissimilar to the ones I had pre-mastectomy, but instead of worrying about no longer having breasts, my self-esteem issues were linked to having extra-large breasts and carrying weight to minimise their size and intrusiveness.

I do believe we all want immediate acceptance from a partner, but we are all so damn good at sabotaging that acceptance purely because we are caught in that cycle of linking our self-esteem to what someone else thinks or has determined as normal or beautiful, a behavioural pattern I had spent much energy learning to breathe through and retrain. But here I was. No boobs. By choice, in a roundabout way. And I was starting that crazy thought process once again. You know the one: 'People will only accept me, be romantically interested in me, based solely on my physical appearance.' What was I doing?

Luckily for me, the penny did drop—well, it crashed, actually. I was at a football game post-mastectomy, wearing my prostheses, and no support BFF by my side. It's not the first game I'd been to alone. In fact, it's rare for me to attend games with someone else, as I used to work on the sidelines as part of team management. But there I was, alone, my prostheses looming large in my peripheral vision.

I can all but guarantee that not a single person would have noticed me on this day for my return to the football sideline post-mastectomy. It was a momentous occasion for me, but seriously, no one took a second glance. Except me. I noticed me. And I certainly noticed my fake breasts.

This football game wasn't some random event. I was attending a game of the team I used to run all the media for back in the day. My previous breasts and I were well known. So all my brain could focus on was how everyone would be noticing how small my breasts were now.

They truly weren't noticing. But my perception was that every single person at the game was looking at me. The anxiety smacked me like a bus. I didn't last the whole game. I avoided eye contact with everyone, and I especially avoided physical contact with anyone who may have known me before. I simply didn't have the strength to answer any questions, and I had it my head that *everyone* would ask questions.

Two decisions were made that day, life-changing decisions with different outcomes but completely entwined consequences: no more prostheses and I shall be forever single. This was possibly the most poignant, liberating and saddest moment in my whole odyssey, and I had not really processed everything appropriately to come to one of those decisions, let alone both.

My choice to ditch the prostheses was the beginning of my new life, the start of me celebrating my uniqueness. It was the day I finally chose to stay flat, completely flat, permanently.

This one seemingly simple action had a profound effect on my self-esteem and self-worth. It was the moment I reminded myself I was unique. I had never fit into the cookie-cutter mould of normal, so why was I attempting to push the proverbial square peg into a round hole just because my world had taken a huge stage-left detour and I was now the owner of a bilateral mastectomy?

And as simple as that, I felt suddenly free. I was at the point where I felt my self-esteem and self-worth could handle any social situation, and the simple change for my brain was not wearing the prostheses that I was worried everyone could notice. I was embracing life without prostheses and rocking it! Some folks may have even suggested I was 'putting myself out there'. I can guarantee I wasn't, as I had made that other decision too. And perhaps in a way this was just as freeing, because I had relieved myself of the potential for incredibly awkward conversations. Well, what I thought would be incredibly awkward conversations, anyway. I do love being wrong.

And this is where I started to discover that it doesn't matter. It's that simple. It truly doesn't matter. I chose not to wear prostheses as I didn't feel the need to hide my lack of cleavage. It doesn't define me, and yet I was allowing it to. So, if someone approaches me, or finds me fascinating or attractive and wants to get to know me more, they already know the shape they're getting. And when did any form of relationship become about someone's shape, anyway? And if it is, I am so not interested—never have been, never will be.

A few months after I had made that seemingly immediate decision to no longer wear prostheses, to stay flat permanently and to live life as a crazy cat lady, the universe threw me a challenge without me even realising it. She quite literally dropped my life partner at my front door. There was magic in the air that day.

There was some work being done on the apartment block I was living in, and the body corporate was showing folks around our building. On this particular day, I'd just got back from the physio and was all taped up, trying to keep my ribs in place, and there was a knock on my apartment's door. Now, this was slightly weird, as it is a secure building, so I figured it was a neighbour. It wasn't.

Apartment doors are huge, heavy fire doors and not easy to open when one is taped from chest to spine. I may have made a statement of pain (I swore loudly) as I pulled the door open to find the bloke who was being shown around our building by the body corporate standing in front of me. He simply said, 'Ouch. I felt that!' I found out much later that he didn't mean the pain I was exuding at the time. Within thirty minutes of meeting me he knew why I was taped up, we'd made hilarious jokes about my lack of breasts, my prostheses falling out in the pool while I was swimming (yes, this happened) and my ever-moving ribs, and he was still laughing as he was in the elevator going down to the next floor. We started our relationship five months later.

As a starting point, I couldn't have been more wrong about how awkward it would be to tell the person you are dating you no longer have breasts and that they've chosen to not grow back. Self-esteem issues do rear their ugly head every now and then—I *am* human—but I always go back to that door moment, when I actually heard my intuition, my inner knowing, finally. I knew we had shared values, and that it was safe for me to be my unique self with him.

And to be honest, at the time it didn't even occur to me I'd just had what I thought was going to be the toughest conversation in the whole odyssey. What did occur to me was, after everything I had faced during the odyssey, it was as simple as changing my mindset, valuing my self-worth and celebrating my uniqueness.

And as suddenly as those onerous 'That's it! Never again for me' dark clouds appeared, they dissipated, as I accepted myself for being elegantly authentic and no longer allowed something that happened to me define me and my future.

My wish is that my experience is used to buoy others who have allowed their dark cloud of perpetual aloneness to envelop them. From my point of view, don't deny others your beauty and uniqueness simply because of an event that happened to you. Yes, it's life-changing. I can only suggest using this to focus on being the you-est you can be. The joy and laughter will certainly follow.

Using woo-woo to get you through

It was these decisions and the complete turning upside down of my 'never again' statement that led to yet another massive emotional and psychological turning point for me. It led me to finally pulling everything I have learnt and know to be true for me together into a single emotional toolkit. I call it my Elegantly Unique Toolkit.

As women, we are conditioned to believe we need to look a certain way, behave a certain way, speak a certain way, flutter eyelashes a certain way, etc. We mostly conform, even if unintentionally, to fit in, to feel valued, to feel visible, to feel worthy of love and to receive external validation for our existence. External validation is definitely important for keeping up our levels of serotonin and dopamine, but our internal validation is twice as important. And when I say 'internal validation', yes, I am referring to the esoteric concept of self-love.

The term 'self-love' has never resonated with me. For me it's like wearing pastel pink—I just don't do it. And yes, for anyone who knows colours, thank you for picking up the direct correlation. But it's the *term* that doesn't resonate, not the actual concept. My preference is to refer to this concept as 'being at one and at peace with your own soul and being, and celebrating your own uniqueness'. For me it's about developing an admiration for yourself, what you have achieved, what you have survived and what values you uphold.

I do recognise these days with the massive shift in our global collective consciousness that the concept is morphing from self-love to self-care, which I feel resonates better with more people and is being instilled from a younger age, and I am truly grateful for this on all counts. I discovered that, in my age group specifically, we have needed a universal smack to bring our attention to looking after ourselves. Generally, this is after incredible emotional upheaval and/or trauma, when the scars have formed and the concrete barriers are well established.

Investing in yourself and developing a life you don't feel the need to escape from gives so much. It gives you an even greater ability for resilience, as well as increasing your knowledge base to navigate your personal odyssey. For me, it ultimately provides the ability to look at the world upside down when you need to find the best solution for you.

I am quite well known for making the following statement to anyone who is doubting the value of self-care or investing in their own peace and joy: 'Only when you are the best version of yourself can you serve and assist others more.' You are truly not being selfish by investing in yourself and wanting to be the best version of you possible.

The next question is, how do you do this without feeling selfish? Once again, one size simply does not fit all. There are so many options available to you to develop your own Elegantly Unique Toolkit.

As I mentioned previously, my toolkit is filled to the brim with my favourite things, which work for me. Some of the strategies I engage are:

- ♥ singing and playing music to diffuse anxiety
- ♥ using colour to enhance moods or decrease anxiety, whether this is clothing, environment or food
- ♥ automatic or free writing. If this is new to you, think journalling while meditating
- ♥ meditating every day
- ♥ mindful breathing exercises. My favourite is four count: breath in for four, hold for four, breath out for eight.
- ♥ practising Reiki every day and follow the Reiki principles as my daily practise

- ♥ movement and exercise every day, mixing it up from walking to pilates to strength or even chakra balancing dancing—whatever it is, I just make sure I move every day!
- ♥ embracing my values and being mindful in my use of language
- ♥ laughing every day
- ♥ Tarot and oracle cards, shiny rocks and pendulums

As I said, these are my favourite tools. They don't have to resonate with everyone, or anyone in fact. Just me. You will note, however, that there are activities missing that many people declare to be the keys to finding peace and practising self-love, such as an activity called mirror work or simply crying. These are not part of my toolkit, as they fall into the 'wearing pastel pink' category. This doesn't diminish their value in any way, it simply reiterates that you should find what works best for you, and please don't feel obliged to use a technique because someone told you it was the best, or 'that's what all counsellors are using right now'. You know your mind, body and spirit better than anyone, if you choose to listen. So use the tools that resonate with you, and you alone.

I continue to undertake important self-discovery and validation work, and personally love metaphorically hanging upside down most days to see all the options available before deciding. In fact, for those Tarot buffs among you, the Hanged Man is one of my most favoured cards!

This inner work is the key to being able to give to yourself and others, as well as the ability to receive in life, and for me was instrumental in unpacking and debunking my second profound statement, 'that's it for me!' let alone navigating the potential awkward conversations about my lack of breasts. As I have shared, the universe had other ideas.

By being able to feel supported through my choice of toolkit activities, the seemingly simple act of choosing to no longer wear prostheses became a truly cathartic moment, and the subsequent unpacking of what that decision meant for my mind, body and spirit led me down a liberating path. I was truly free. Not only was I free to wear a plethora of off-the-shoulder numbers, as I no longer wear a bra or any form of undergarment-top-thingy, but I was also free to follow my values and suddenly understood what I would no longer accept in life and relationships. This was key for me in re-establishing my belief in myself, my self-worth and my self-esteem.

I really do encourage anyone to take the time to do this, to find what makes up your Elegantly Unique Toolkit. Take time to establish or re-establish your values and re-ignite your self-worth. Whether you seek professional assistance or are able to achieve this yourself, just do it. When you do, there is no end to the possibilities you can achieve through your increased confidence and self-worth. Yes, you may even be able to have that sticky conversation without even realising you were having it. I did.

It truly is a never-ending story

Where does all this inner-work, ignoring inner-knowing, acceptance of uniqueness, a-ha moments, life decisions, metaphorically hanging upside down, pondering—and the list goes on—actually end? Simple: it doesn't. It wouldn't be living if it did.

Your story is never-ending. And for those of us extra woo-woo folk, it truly is never-ending. Never stop learning or growing or questioning, and remember to implement all your newly found knowingness.

For me, I am hoping to use all I have discovered and am still discovering to assist other unique, elegantly rebellious souls. And in developing that plan I have been doing some very non-P-A things, and have been reminded that life is one big learning event, and we are never at the end of learning, either, no matter how much inner-work or work you feel you have achieved. There is always more.

For example, I recently decided I needed to have photos taken for my business idea and book. By doing this, I found out I still had stuff to learn.

I stumbled across an amazing photographer, Mel Watt, and chose to have a session with her. It turned out to be the most awe-inspiring decision I have made throughout the odyssey.

Not only is Mel an incredible photographer who uses her artistic talents to raise funds for the McGrath Foundation, but she was able to capture my quirky uniqueness in film and encourage my unique sense of fun throughout the whole empowering experience. It was during the shoot when Mel made the following statement to me: 'How does it feel using your book idea to be the voice for other mastectomy ladies?'

I do believe there is a photo of me pondering this statement. *Being someone else's voice.* I hadn't thought of it that way. And this was the part that caused me to continue pondering.

I am not a voice for others. Nope, that's not how I roll. As an introvert, I couldn't think of anything more challenging, in fact. Even a 'topless' photo of my scars by a total stranger wasn't as challenging as the thought of being someone else's voice.

I also don't feel I want the responsibility of someone handing their power over to me, because for me this is exactly what this means.

My dream and wish is to be able to inspire others to find their voices. To take up their space. To stand in their personal power. To ask their questions. To believe in their version of normal. To find their version of truth. To be able to disrupt society's version of normal, should they choose. To discover their uniqueness. To celebrate their whole being, mind, body, spirit and soul.

And, above all, as owners of a mastectomy, to be able to voice how they choose to live their lives as the best version they can be, whether that is staying flat, reconstructed or prosthesis-upped. To be able to live their version of freedom through their individual choices.

Mel's seemingly innocuous statement pushed me into action once again. It is a moment I am forever grateful for. In that moment Mel reminded me of my passion and my why.

It was also a reminder that the odyssey is truly a never-ending story.

Every day you can have an 'oh, that's right' moment. Whether this is when trying on clothes and something just doesn't sit quite right anymore, or moving slightly the incorrect way and popping a rib. (I recently stubbed my left little toe and started to fall over. Instinctively I threw my right arm up in the air to balance myself, which resulted in pulling on mastectomy scar tissue and popping a couple of ribs. It truly can be that simple.) Or the plethora of ongoing appointments as a consequence of continued recovery. Or having to jump up from the computer mid-thought, all because your scar tissue and body are screaming at you for typing just that little bit longer than it wanted you to, i.e., twenty-two minutes is just too long! Or taking over four years to write a book simply because your body has physical limitations that turn two hours of writing into five hours of activity with all the stretching and moving ribs around. Or having medical professionals asking you often if 'you've changed your mind about staying flat after all'.

And as I often say to folks, none of this is either good or bad, it is simply different. Bottom line: trauma changes us. It affects us in ways we do not expect and cannot plan for. A cancer diagnosis is trauma. It truly is that simple. Recovery takes compassion *from* yourself and others, as well as *for* yourself and others. It also takes determination, inner-strength and knowing.

Everyone's diagnosis, treatment and recovery are completely different. It is up to us as unique individuals to embrace this and focus on being the best version of our stylish and authentic selves.

My lived experience is just that, uniquely mine. I am a bilateral-mastectomy owner who has chosen to stay flat. I am not a single-mastectomy owner. I didn't have chemo. I'm not a transgender male who had a bilateral to truly be their authentic self (folks I am most in awe of, by the way) and I cannot tell you about what it's like to lose your hair due to treatment.

What I can say from my lived experience is *embrace all the changes*. The things I have achieved or changed subsequent to having a breast cancer diagnosis and bilateral mastectomy even I don't believe some days.

- ♥ I was medically retired from a career I loved, but I found my passion and how I can be of service through sharing my knowledge and lived experiences.
- ♥ I have dodgy limbs, popping ribs, and live with pain all day, every day, but I was introduced to the world of exercise physiology, fascial muscle groups and the lymphatic

system, and have gained so much strength and fitness as well as achieving three charity walks to date, something I can guarantee wouldn't have appeared in my former self's purview.

♥ I have a tattoo. Yes, me, little Miss Victorian Sensibilities. After deciding to not have reconstruction, I was planning on having my scars tattooed, a brilliant concept for us extra-unique folks. This plan was knocked on the head by my clinicians. This was the saddest day of my whole odyssey, in fact. But there was good sciencey reasons. So, I still got my tattoo, just on my back. It was sort of like the mirror version of what I had planned, if you will. And I love it. It represents 'from mud comes beauty and enlightenment'—yes, stylishly authentic.

♥ I used to do everything humanly possible to hide myself and my breasts, and I avoided having photos done at all costs, and

I have now done a full photo shoot, no makeup, with topless scar shots and all. PS: I highly recommend such photoshoots. And, in fact, if you scan the code in the following pic there's a thank you gift from Mel Watt Photography.

♥   I have never accepted society's version of normal. However, I subconsciously allowed society to define my version of myself, and I would hide to avoid not fitting in. And now I proudly take up space and have no qualms whatsoever accepting that not fitting into the world's version of normal is exactly how I fit into my life.

♥   I used to internalise my questions and not voice my thoughts out of fear of being seen as having a unique view. Now I celebrate my uniqueness 110 percent.

If I can achieve one more thing, it would be for this little coffee chat in a book to be someone else's turning point in finding their own voice to ask questions, to point out when they are not being asked the questions directly when others are making assumptions based a general concept of normal.

As I said at the beginning of this chat, this is *my* story, my lived experience and some of the things I have instigated to celebrate my elegantly, stylishly, authentic version of uniqueness for me, not society.

I do truly look forward to the day when we all celebrate our individual uniqueness and are accepted for the choices we make for ourselves to be the best we can be. Always remember to celebrate you as a person. Honour you as a person. Respect you as a person. Love you as a person. That's your version of uniquely normal.

It really is that simple for me. And, naturally, I also wish for world peace.

Bonus: PeAchy blah-blah recipes

Recipes from the wisdom and ponderings of PeAchy the Owl

PeAchy blah-blah chocolate

Ingredients

- ♥ 3 tablespoons coconut oil, melted
- ♥ 2 tablespoons rice malt syrup
- ♥ 1 tablespoon almond butter or tahini
- ♥ I heaped tablespoon cacao
- ♥ Splash of vanilla extract

Method

Place the coconut oil, rice malt syrup and almond butter or tahini into a microwave-safe container. Melt for about 30 seconds just so they start to blend together. Be careful not to overheat. These ingredients need to be melted, not heated.

Then whisk or stir the melted ingredients together until they are blended thoroughly and resemble a caramel consistency.

Add the cacao and vanilla (or other flavour, such as peppermint or ginger, if you like) and mix well. It should be a similar consistency to ganache.

You can add pepitas, sunflower seeds, sesame seeds or toasted coconut flakes for crunch now if you like.

Pour the mixture into a baking-paper-lined 20 cm x 5 cm container. Refrigerate until solid—takes a couple of hours to be truly solid. Then cut into bite-size pieces and store in a sealed container in the fridge. Eat and enjoy.

Top tip: Basically the ratio is 3:2:1:1. Meaning 3 measures of coconut oil melted, 2 of rice malt syrup, 1 of cacao, 1 of almond butter or tahini and a splash of vanilla for good measure. Use this recipe's measurements as a starting point and have fun working out what tastes best for you.

PeAchy's blah-blah caramel slice

Ingredients

Base

- ♥ 1 cup buckwheat flour
- ♥ ⅓ cup coconut sugar
- ♥ ¼ cup desiccated coconut
- ♥ ⅓ cup coconut oil, melted

Filling

- ♥ 6 tablespoons nut butter or tahini
- ♥ 4 tablespoons rice malt syrup
- ♥ 4 tablespoons coconut oil, melted
- ♥ 3 tablespoons coconut cream
- ♥ 1 teaspoon vanilla extract
- ♥ pinch of salt

Top layer

- ♥ 6 tablespoons cacao or cocoa powder
- ♥ 4 tablespoons coconut oil, liquid
- ♥ 2 tablespoons rice malt syrup

Method

Preheat oven to 180°C/160°C fan-forced. Grease an 18 cm x 28 cm slice pan. Line base and sides with baking paper, extending paper 2 cm above edges of pan.

Place buckwheat flour, brown sugar, desiccated coconut and the coconut oil in a bowl. Stir until well combined. Press coconut mixture evenly over the base of prepared pan. Bake until a light golden colour, about 20 minutes. Set aside to completely cool.

Once the base is cooled, place the ingredients for the filling into your processor and blend at medium speed until the mixture is smooth and well combined. Try to avoid over-blending, as the ingredients may spilt. Pour the mixture over your base and place in the fridge to set.

Once the filling layer is set, mix the ingredients together for your chocolate topping. Make sure the coconut oil is melted but not hot. When mixed, pour the topping over your slice, spreading it out to cover the filling layer. Place the slice in the fridge to set.

Serve. Eat and enjoy! You may wish to place the slice into the freezer for 20 minutes prior to slicing. Once sliced, this can be stored and served straight from the fridge or freezer. It will not be stable at room temperature.

Note: An alternative topping is:
- ♥ 200g dairy-free dark chocolate, chopped (see notes)
- ♥ 1 tablespoon coconut oil

To make this topping, place chocolate and coconut oil in a microwave-safe bowl. Microwave on high (100%), stirring halfway through, for 1 minute or until melted and smooth. Working quickly, pour chocolate mixture over filling layer, spreading to cover to the edges. Place the slice in the fridge to set.

PeAchy's zucchini and ginger 'bread'

Makes 10–12 slices/muffins

Ingredients

- ♥ 2 cups almond meal or LSA[4] or mixture of 1:1
- ♥ 1 teaspoon cinnamon
- ♥ 2 teaspoons ground ginger
- ♥ 1 teaspoon gluten-free baking powder
- ♥ ½ teaspoon sea salt
- ♥ 1 cup zucchini, unpeeled and grated (about 1 large zucchini)
- ♥ ¼ cup coconut oil or non-dairy spread
- ♥ ¼ cup rice malt syrup
- ♥ 2 free-range eggs
- ♥ Sunflower seeds and pepitas (optional)

Method

Preheat oven to 180°C.

Combine almond meal/LSA, cinnamon, ginger and baking powder in a bowl. Add zucchini, coconut oil and rice malt and stir thoroughly. Add eggs and mix well.

Pour into a lightly greased or lined bread tin or spoon into muffin cases. Top with sunflower seeds and pepitas if you so desire. Bake until golden on top and inserted skewer comes out clean. (muffins about 25 mins; loaf about 35 mins, depending on your oven, of course).

Can be served warm with a light spread of dairy-free butter or lactose-free cream cheese for the extra adventurous, or at room temp, i.e., lunch boxes.

---

4   ground linseed (flaxseed), sunflower seeds and almonds

Get to know P-A

Firstly, thank you so much for taking the time to read my wee odyssey. I truly hope you were able to find some useful information and even a few a-ha moments of your own along the way.

This is my first foray into the world of publishing, and didn't I choose quite a disruptive topic to kick things off. And because I am well known for having a coffee and a natter, my writing style is intentionally akin to hanging out and having a cuppa with me.

From a background point of view, I've been blessed to have spent most of my life living in beautiful Queensland, Australia. I started this life in the Sunshine Coast region, then moved to Far North Queensland and finally back to the south-east corner.

Writing and asking 'but why?' has always been my thing, whether that was at school, university or my career. In fact, it is purported the first real statement I made at the age of eighteen months was exactly that—but why? Clearly I was an unconventional conventionalist from the get go!

I have also loved all things woo-woo most of my life. From the age of about seventeen I started my love affair with reading cards. I even made my first set of personal Oracle Cards when I was nineteen. I have also been drawn to the energy of very shiny rocks—meaning crystals— from a very early age too.

Interestingly though, I'm not that person who kept a diary or a daily journal. For me this approach becomes task driven and lacks the freedom to do what you want when it's best for you. Strangely I do journal, but only for the cards I pull. And although I pull cards every day, I only journal on days when my memory is really choosing to be challenging! Yes this is the conundrum that is P-A!!!

So when I was medically retired in 2019 from a career I loved, working for law enforcement and emergency services, it was no great surprise to me that my writing lead me back to my more esoteric path of holistic counselling, Reiki, colour therapy and soul coaching.

It's been through my writing that I rediscovered my main passion in life has always been to assist people find the positives in all situations and to be of service. I love being able to assist people in rediscovering their authentic self, and realising the answers are always within them—buried most of the time, but still there.

It won't be a surprise to anyone that *Alice in Wonderland* and *Peter Pan*—think about my name, jussayin'—were my two favourite books as a child and still are at fifty-two! These books are filled with curiosity and unlimited possibilities and lots of giggling at life and its obscurities.

I firmly believe my love for these works is why I am one of those very curious souls who chooses to laugh at the challenges life throws us, as opposed to crying, and who looks for all possibilities in the seemingly impossible situation. I have a proclivity to look at life upside-down if you will. And to the chagrin of many, I am literally that person who sees the moonrise every day or the sunset and is still amazed by it every single time.

My somewhat whimsical approach to life can be quite annoying to some on occasion, however I have learnt acceptance is the key to understanding everyone's individual life adventures and odysseys. I am also incredibly adept at shapeshifting to meet whatever situation I find myself in. My career was an amazing example of this—a high functioning, highly sensitive, introvert working in the media and public relations arena. I can guarantee any of my former colleagues would laugh loudly if I said I was actually an introvert!

I am over the moon about the next stage of my adventure and assisting like-minded souls with rediscovering their uniqueness and celebrating all that they are and can be.

As the Cheshire Cat declared, *"Every adventure requires a first step."*

Writing *What Happens When They Don't Grow Back* is my first step. Are you ready to take your first step? I would love to hear all about it or even assist you take the first steps.

If you're ready to celebrate you as a person. Honour you as a person. Respect you as a person. Love you as a person—and take 100% responsibility for ALL of it. Let's get you started. Reach out to me through *www.peta-annwood.au*.

References

Jolie A. Doggett: *What People with Big Boobs Want You to Know*: Huffington Post; September 23, 2019

Myjanne Jensen: *Opinion: I was going to get breast implants. Here's what changed my mind:* Earshot: ABC Radio National; March 18, 2021

Rowan Martin: *Getting it off my chest: life with big breasts*: The Guardian (online); November 14, 2015

Cancer Australia: canceraustralia.gov.au: *Recurrent and metastatic cancer*: accessed December 2021

Breast Cancer Network Australia: bcna.org.au: *Exercise and staying fit*: accessed December 2021

The Gait Guys: thegaitguys.com: *Human Gait Changes Following Mastectomy*: tumblr.com: 2013

National Breast Cancer Foundation: nbcf.org.au

Gok Wan: gokwan.com

Fluid Health Co: fluidhealthco.com.au

Seed Physiotherapy: seedphysio.com.au

Pinc & Steel: au.pincandsteel.com

Wellness for Women: wellnessforwomenclinic.com

Mel Watt Photography: www.melwattphotography.com.au

Emmaus Health & Wellness: emmaushealthandwellness.com.au

The Quiet Collective: quietcollective.com.au

Stand Tall AFC: standtallafc.org

Not Putting on a Shirt: notputtingonashirt.org

www.ingramcontent.com/pod-product-compliance
Lightning Source LLC
Chambersburg PA
CBHW050953050726
47592CB00007B/2551